# THE OSARO THEORY

Efosa Osaro

Grosvenor House
Publishing Limited

The right of Efosa Osaro to be identified as the author of this
work has been asserted in accordance with Section 78
of the Copyright, Designs and Patents Act 1988

The book cover is copyright to Efosa Osaro

This book is published by
Grosvenor House Publishing Ltd
Link House
140 The Broadway, Tolworth, Surrey, KT6 7HT.
www.grosvenorhousepublishing.co.uk

A CIP record for this book
is available from the British Library

ISBN 978-1-78623-531-2

DEDICATED TO: EFOSA JUNIOR OSARO

Hope this may serve you as a map to navigate
the world with a better understanding.
Cherish it with Love, Peace and Kindness.

# CHAPTERS

# ACKNOWLEDGMENTS

I want to record my heartfelt thanks to the writers and authors who served as guides and inspiration for the creation of this book.

My most profound gratitude to the Reverend Jeremiah Wright, Dr. Ani Marimba, Chance Kelsey's files, Daniel Goleman, Thom Hartmann, Gary Lachman, and Iain McGilchrist.

# INTRODUCTION

I was born into a family of five children, in a single parent household. My early years were spent in a small town, in the local government area of Benin City, Nigeria, where my parents lived for most of their lives. My brother, my older sister, and I slept in a tiny room with little or no furniture, a blue carpet, and a wobbly creaky double bed. Sometimes I slept on the floor to allow me freedom to stretch and sleep comfortably, which was not easy when sharing with my siblings.

My grandmother named me Efosa, which means the "wealth of God", and my last name adds more weight to my shoulders; Osaro means "there is God". Even though I did not fully grasp the significance of my name, I always believed in it. Having such a name, though, did not change much in my life or the conditions we were living in at that time.

From a very young age through to adulthood, I've always believed that anything, I repeat anything, is possible. As long as you have faith and belief, you will be able to move mountains by simply taking the first step: action!

That was what I had, and it helped me to step into the world with the right approach and attitude. For the past 15 years, I have been on this journey called life, with the hunger not for food but for knowledge. I went in search of knowledge and answers to questions that no-one seemed to care about. I have always wondered if the hard conditions we find spread across sub-Saharan Africa were truly caused by poverty. It seems to me that there is a different reason, something deeper, embedded in the African struggle.

In my pursuit of knowledge to fully grasp the struggle of my people and to understand why Africans till this day believe that the solution and the cause of their problems is Europe, I've travelled and visited many countries from Sweden to the United States of America, and lived in three different European countries – Italy, the Netherlands, and the United Kingdom.

I realized that all black people, from the motherland Africa to all African descendants across the globe, possess a different kind of intelligence. This undiscovered intelligence is the core of the African problem and the only solution to their issues.

This book you're about to read is a testimony of my life, which proves that anything is possible. Because when you change the way you look at things, the things you look at change.

The Osaro Theory suggests that the intelligence of black people slightly differs from that of Europeans. Black people are right-brain dominant compared to Europeans, who are left-brain orientated. The right-brain trait has helped blacks to thrive and succeed despite the hardship of racial condition throughout history. This core intelligence, which is genetic as well as social and cultural, has helped blacks to procreate culture that has impacted and influenced our modern world. Their influence has shaped the world of art, music, sport, style, fashion and entertainment.

The lack of awareness of this form of intelligence has caused black nations to be under-developed and to underachieve, compare to the First World; this is also "the gift and the curse" that has paralyzed sub-Saharan Africa from being able to realize its full potential. One of the world's most eminent scientists, James Watson, claimed that Africans are less intelligent than Westerners and that the idea of equal power of reason shared across racial groups was a delusion.

As an African born in Nigeria and raised in a Western world, I do not believe in racism or in racial supremacy. I believe in equality in every aspect of general intelligence. In my book, I have observed that when it comes to intelligence, some people tend to use certain parts of the brain more than others; this is due to their cultural heritage and the geographical climate where they evolved.

So, in order for Africa to grow and develop, it must first identify and embrace its true core of intelligence, which I discovered and refer to as the EMOTIONAL RESERVOIR.

# CHILDHOOD DAYS

Born into a family of five children and raised in a single-parent household, I always wondered why my mother had to work extra hard to raise us on her own. Sometimes it was hard for her to find money for groceries after the household bills were paid, while we also had outstanding school fees and no transport money.

The economic collapse in the late 1970s and early 1980s contributed to substantial discontent in the country, and the conflict between ethnic communities and nationalities added to the political pressure, resulting in the Nigerian government expelling more than 2 million illegal workers (mostly from Ghana, Niger, Cameroon, and Chad). Based on the 1987 data, for the first time, the World Bank declared Nigeria as a low-income country and poor enough to be eligible for aid from the International Development Association[1].

As a result, many Nigerian families started looking overseas to seek a better life, and when I was two years old, my mother left us in Nigeria and went to find a new home in the province of Naples, Italy.

Living with my aunt was the best part of my childhood. From the age of seven I began to partake in household responsibilities. My job was to fetch clean water and to make sure that there was always water in the house for cooking and drinking. I still remember the first time my aunty told me that it was my turn to go and fetch clean water. Getting clean water in the city where I was born was not quite easy, due to the shortage of water wells and boreholes in the neighborhood. I had to walk ten miles away from home, with a twenty-liter container, in search of water. So if I had a one hundred-liter tank of water to fill up for that day, it meant I had to make that journey five times!

Despite having to walk so far, I found it enjoyable because it was an opportunity to catch up with my friends who were also in the same water struggle as me. It gave us a chance to talk about everything from our favorite cars and movies, to homework from school.

My aunty did the best she could to raise us properly so that we didn't end up on the streets or become caught up in the street activities. In my community at that time, having a member of family living overseas was like winning the lottery, as not everyone had the opportunity to move out to search for a better life elsewhere. I remember I had to lie when a friend asked me where my mother was, but they later found out that she was living in Italy. In some ways I was proud that my mother was living in Europe, but part of me hated the fact that she was not there to look after me, my brother, and sister.

I finished my primary school and graduated to Junior Secondary School, where I had to walk miles to get to school in time. We had to study more European history in school, and less African history. By then, I knew where England was on the map and countries like France, Germany, Holland, Sweden, and Italy were memorized by heart and their history was taught and written in text books.

The school system was built on the European way of education, where we were taught to speak French and English. The vernacular we spoke was regarded as "bad" language and inferior, so we weren't allowed to speak it in school. Africa's inferiority was drilled into us in almost every class we entered, and in almost every book we studied[2].

At school, learning was hard for me, because I couldn't understand why they taught us so much of European history and so few topics about Africa. Although I was learning new things, my main interest was to find out about the history of Africa, why the Europeans came, and why we had to study more of their history at school and less about ours. At the age of eleven, the only things I knew about Africa and my native country, Nigeria, were the states and the capital city (Abuja). The highest mountain in Africa, Mount Kilimanjaro, was part of a song we recited all the time during the school recreational break.

On the long walk back home with my friends, we discussed Europe and things my mother had said about the snow and the cold weather. It was fascinating and hard to ignore how popular and respected I became because my mother was living in Italy.

Once she had finally settled and found a job in Naples, we started receiving money from her on monthly basis, and this improved our economical situation. People looked at us as privileged because of the clothes we wore, our school bags, and the electronic gadgets we had, because the average family couldn't afford to purchase these items for their kids.

I enjoyed visiting my grandmother, who lived near us, because it helped me to find out about my family. One day, while visiting her after school, she told me that my mother and father had split up after I was born. I was very upset to learn that this was the reason why my mother was working so hard, and that she had left in search of a better life in another country in order to provide for us.

I was also very curious to know more about Africa and its people, but my grandmother agreed to discuss this with me if I helped her to fetch firewood. Though my back was hurting from gathering firewood, the story of Africa was more important to me than anything else. She told me stories about the British Empire, when the British arrived in Nigeria for the first time, and how slavery and colonization started in West Africa. Sadly, when I was just twelve years old, my grandmother passed away after a long-term illness.

My aunty was getting ready to travel abroad with the help of my mother. So, my brother, sister and I had to relocate to the city where my uncle lived. As a DJ, he had a huge record collection in his house, and one of my favorite album covers was that of Fela Kuti. The artwork had some funny pictures of black people in chains, and leaders of Europe dividing Africa. I never understood the meaning until I was lucky enough to hear the record, *Follow Follow*, which made me realize that we Africans needed to learn our history first before following that of the white man.

For the first time, I questioned why African history was hidden? Why is it that Africa was so poor and Europe so rich? Why were our people insecure about their own history? These thoughts were always in the back of my mind, but I couldn't understand because nobody was there to educate me. Yet they remained in my little brain.

The dream to travel to Europe and America was in the heart of all Africans. Millions were unemployed, homeless, and impoverished by bad governance, which left young people no choice but to take all the risks necessary to travel abroad. The irresponsibility of African leaders who were unable to govern properly, made everyone believe that corruption was deeper in the roots of the country. From the bus driver, driving his hired bus to make a living; to the market woman selling anything she could to feed her family; to the unpaid pensioner; to the low-paid teachers in the schools and universities – corruption was felt and seen by the naked eyes.

The African youth who would be the future leaders, scientists, economists, doctors, nurses, and engineers, were desperately moving elsewhere to chase their dreams. The older generation, whose responsibility was to protect and cherish, left young Africans with no hope for a better life and encouraged them to disperse across the world.

Gaining a visa was difficult, though, and many lied about their reason for travelling out of the country. Those who couldn't get a visa or weren't financially able, started to search for an easier way to leave the country. Many took different routes to cross from one border to another until they reached the coast of Spain or Italy. I remember hearing about some of my friends' uncles, fathers, and sisters, who died in the Mediterranean Sea while trying to cross into Europe. In our case, because we had a member of our family living there, travel to Europe wasn't seen as impossible. We knew that one day we might get the opportunity to visit.

When my aunty left, my uncle became the new beneficiary of money being sent from abroad. When it arrived, my uncle would invite his friends over and we would have parties with a lot of food and drink. My uncle never bothered to invest some of the money into small businesses, or to save for rainy days. Instead, we would just party and enjoy ourselves until the money ran out, then go back to being hungry again.

This pathological behavior was inevitable and had become a routine that I never understood. While my brother and sister spent their pocket money buying things they didn't really need, I opened my first saving account to save my meagre pocket money. I even saved my school transport allowance, by walking to school.

My account generated a little interest, to the point where my uncle would often borrow from me and repay whenever we received money again from abroad.

Having relatives in Europe was becoming a common thing in the community; in every third house, there was someone who was providing them with financial support from abroad. Suddenly, competition grew and became about who was wearing the best clothes, who was building the biggest house, and who was riding the fastest car. I found myself getting caught up in arguments and bragging about material things. Although they didn't really matter much to me, I felt I had to boast about them so that I would not be isolated from my circle of friends.

I always hoped that those living in Europe would come back to educate our people and possibly bring new ideas that could help improve the living condition in our community. But instead they returned to show off about the life they lived in Europe, to brag about how much their wristwatches and cars cost, and to announced that they no longer belonged to Africa, because they enjoy the lifestyle abroad.

I still remember the first time my friend's sister came back from Europe. The whole community knew she was around, because they always partied. This behavior just fueled the desire of our people and poor families who didn't have pride, to travel to Europe by any means.

I started to believe that maybe Europe was Heaven. Seeing a picture of Jesus as a white man, hanging on the walls of churches, made me question why the African system of worship was looked at as inferior. Was the white man's religion superior?

Eight months from my thirteenth birthday, I was admitted to hospital for two months. I underwent surgery and had the right side of my mouth stitched.

A few weeks after the operation, my uncle came to visit and told me that my mum would be coming soon, because of my injury. I was happy to hear the good news, but at the same time I was sad because I would not be able to stay with her and ask her all the questions I wanted to know about Europe.

It was the Wednesday afternoon and I had taken my medication that morning, so I slept. As soon as I woke up, I could feel the presence of somebody standing by my bedside and I could smell a very beautiful perfume in the room. I opened my eyes and saw my mother. I was so happy that I jumped on her and hugged her tight.

She told me she had to come back home because of my operation, as she was very concerned about me. She stayed with me in the hospital all that day, and I was discharged the following morning. I was still going to be under hospital supervision and would have weekly home visits by the doctors and nurses to check on my health and monitor my recovery.

Coming back home after such a long time, I was excited and couldn't wait to catch up with my friends and family members. Having my mother around, too, was a wonderful feeling. Now I could ask her all the question I wanted to know about Europe and how it felt to live there.

Security in my home town was poor, which led to crime and the activities of street gangs flourished; we often heard rumors of people being kidnapped and killed by armed robbers, and children going missing. Even walking home from school could sometimes be a nightmare, as we couldn't tell who wanted to harm us. It was so bad that people with a lot of money hired police officers to escort them around the city.

I began to see the lack of trust and fear shattering my community, and was really concerned for my mother's safety during her stay. People didn't trust each other any more, so I knew that my home could be at risk and my mother a target of these crimes that was unfolding.

Weeks went by and my mother was getting ready to return to Italy, but before she left, she wanted to visit a lady she knew from our home town. I was excited to travel with her and to meet her friend, even though it meant a bus ride of about 50 minutes.

When we arrived, I could see my mother's body language change; she seemed really nervous. The lady had a beautiful house with a big gate, and it was obvious when we got inside that she was very rich and powerful. She had housekeepers, nannies, and security guards present all the time. I couldn't believe what I was witnessing!

I was offered a cold drink while my mother and the lady went inside a room. While I was enjoying my cold juice, I could hear the woman shouting at my mother. I didn't understand what was going on in there, but suddenly my mother came out of the room looking sad and frustrated and the woman asked us to leave.

On our journey back home, my mother wasn't happy, so I asked her what had happened in that room. She looked at me, smiled, and replied, "Nothing! Nothing happened." But deep down, I knew that there was a problem and something was wrong. She said her priority was for us to one day join her in Europe, so before she left she made some arrangement with my uncle to start applying for our travel passport.

Two months after she went back to Italy, she was granted the documents needed for our visa application. It was great news!

I was excited and looking forward to our trip to the Big City, and I remember wearing a pair of white trousers with a red sweater. The weather was about 38 degrees, but although it was a very hot day, my only concern was to wear the best clothes I had and show off to my friends and the people in my community.

We arrived in Lagos, where the Italian Embassy was located at the time, at around 5pm and stopped by the bus station to buy snacks and water. My uncle had booked a cheap hotel for us overnight, as we had to keep our expenditure to a minimum due to the cost of visas. Our hotel room had just a single bed and a bathroom, so that night I had to sleep on the floor while my uncle and my brother slept in the bed.

We woke early the next morning to start packing our suitcases and get ready for the appointment. After sharing the bathroom, we dressed quickly and checked out to ensure we did not have to pay extra for overstaying.

Lagos was a very busy place where everybody wanted to do business, which made it crowded. And on our journey to the visa appointment, we were caught in the worst traffic jam I have ever witnessed in my life. The rush-hour traffic was so bad that we sat in the car sweating, and drinking a lot of water to stay dehydrated I was soaking wet in my sweater and my white trousers had almost turned into a different color due to the dust and heat. And the sun wasn't going away anytime soon!

After several hours, we made it out of the traffic jam and headed to the Italian Embassy. We had heard they were very strict with appointment times, so we made sure we had our passport photos ready and, luckily, we got there on time and our applications were accepted.

By the time we returned to my home town, my uncle had contacted my mother with the news. She was really happy and couldn't wait to have us with her.

After several more months waiting for a response from the Italian Embassy, we did finally receive our international passports and were also issued with a family visa. We could finally start planning for our trip. I couldn't wait to tell my friends I would be leaving, but my uncle warned me not to tell anyone until the day we planned to travel out of the country. I guess this was something to do with the lack of security that could possibly put our lives in danger. Despite the fears, we invited some friends over and had a big party.

It was a wonderful feeling to know that I was leaving my hometown to join my mother after so many years of separation. But although I was excited to travel to see what Europe had to offer, deep inside I was sad to know that so few families could afford to move out of the poor conditions and seek for a better life elsewhere.

# EUROPE AS IMAGINED

I've always imagined Europe as some sort of a "Heaven on Earth" paradise where people lived happily with nature, or at least, a place where there is no homelessness or hungry people, and where there is peace and tranquility at all time.

Most Africans imagine Europe this way; many see it as a land paved with gold, with many opportunities and chances for them. They believe that they have to come to the promise land, where milk and honey flow, and where money grows on trees.

The obsession of wanting to travel to Europe has left so many Africans brainwashed to the point that it would be hard to tell them otherwise. The so-called "Heaven on Earth" propaganda promoting the white men culture, has always been spread right across the media, from newspapers to textbooks, movies and magazines, all helping to poison the minds of the African people.

Our leaders never taught us to be proud of being African. And when people have no jobs and see no future in Africa, they become obsessed with Europe and America. Some are so desperate that they even travel to Asia and the Middle East looking for something that they can't find in their homeland.

People in my home town were desperate to seek a better life elsewhere, as crime increased. Around the country, people began to sell their land, property, and what little they had, to pay for their children or family members' travel expenses to Europe. Some even took out bank loans to pursue that dream.

Many Africans still see Europe as the only way out of the conditions they live in. I always wondered, if there was no Europe would there be an alternative solution to our problem?

Some educated Black Africans who studied in some of the most prestigious universities in the West, would then return home to continue the legacy of corruption which you could smell in every part of the country. With nothing to offer, this made me always question what African leaders were doing and why there was no sense of direction in our country?

In my home town, street gangs fight and kill for the honor of the street but they never dare to challenge the miserable conditions in which they find themselves. These lives could have had more impact if they died to free the country from the corrupted leaders.

Families with zero income kept on having children, 6 or 7, when they could barely feed themselves. Many died while crossing to the shores of Spain, Lampedusa in Italy, or using the Libyan route where Africans board a boat from the coast of Libya to cross the Mediterranean Sea.

Many have lost their loved ones on this journey, for the sake of seeking a better life elsewhere from their homeland. The refugee crisis in the Mediterranean has already seen so many drowned at sea, and their families never get to bury their corpse. The internet is full of this information, but the young Africans refuse to believe it. They are distrustful and think that these reports only want to destroy their dream for a better life. So they take to the road without money and without knowing what awaits them where they are going.

Just like other Africans who have left their homeland, here I was in Europe. I landed at the Malpensa International Airport in Milan, Italy, overjoyed at the prospect of joining my mother again after so many years. It was a sunny afternoon in mid-April, and we stopped by a restaurant to have some food and drink and enjoy finally being there.

I was curious looking at the beautiful things around me while we waited to be served, but then I began to notice that people were staring at us and keeping their distance. I never thought of it as negative until I started to experience the increased hostility towards Black African in Europe. As Africans, we never thought to distance ourselves from other people because of their race, or to separate ourselves from people who came from a different culture.

From the schools and the places of worship, to the language we spoke, everything helped to Europeanize our African minds and reaffirm the idea that Europe was a place where we could belong! Subconsciously, though, it took away our pride and love for own nation. Yet here, on the other side of the world, the information about Africa centered on pictures of poor children in tents, like savages. Our image was used to create campaigns as if we were some sort of charity cases, and this had a psychological effect on many Africans living in Europe.

Those who found themselves in a new culture, started to experience a general stressful life; many were unable to find a decent job, others complained of discrimination and racism where they lived. Those who came to Europe in search of a better life complained their dream wasn't fulfilled and that they rarely found happiness. Their feelings of stress increased the longer they lived in the country, but yet they still refused to go back. Many suffered from depression, due to endless trouble with immigration laws and constantly facing deportation.

At the beginning, things were rough and difficult for me in Italy. I was the only black in a class of 24 white students from different European backgrounds. I was constantly getting in trouble because I looked different, and couldn't express myself because of the language barrier. My inability to speak Italian got me into many fistfights at school and I often ended up in the Principal's office.

I soon learned the hard way, through confrontation, argument, yelling, and being called "Negro" all the time.

During recreation breaks, the black students sat at one table while the whites students sat separately. A Senegalese national, Chise', later became my friend, and he translated many of the things I didn't understand in Italian.

I asked Chise', "What is the meaning of negro?"

He replied bluntly, "It means nigger!"

I was baffled and shocked that a white person could make such a derogatory remake towards a black person. Though I'd heard

12

about racism before, I had never witnessed it! However, I didn't take it as an insult, because I thought maybe the word "nigger" was just their way of expressing their dislike for me. So I moved on.

After a short period, I started to notice racism manifesting itself more clearly. White kids were calling us monkeys and gorillas, and telling us to go back to Africa. We were bullied in school, harassed on the bus, and bananas were thrown at us. This became part of our daily life.

Chise' and I were frustrated that the white students were never punished for their behavior, and the teachers did very little to stop it. It also made it hard for us to concentrate and focus on our studies, and I was always behind in class assignments and my homework as never submitted on time. The constant distress even caused Chise' to drop out after the first year, in search of employment.

My mother was struggling to keep up with the school tuition fees. As a cleaner, working two jobs, she had to raise us, pay the bills, and still send money back to our family in Africa. So, I decided to pursue employment after I completed my second year of High School. But I had no idea about the struggle facing black people within the job market.

Blacks were less likely to get hired for the same job as whites, due to racism and discrimination. And the struggles and living conditions of the unemployed were unpleasant to see. So many had left their homeland in hope of a better life, yet their dreams had been shattered across every corner of Europe.

I saw a lot of Africans in extreme poverty, despair, and forced to do anything to survive. Some became homeless, or drug dealers, while others were forced into prostitution, which they found difficult to break free from. I was reminded of the rich lady who my mother visited when she came back to Africa to visit. It turned out that the lady was called 'MADAME', and was well known and respected amongst the Nigerian community, responsible for sponsoring young girls and women to Europe and promising them wonderful things.

Those back home were not aware of what was going on, because many were too proud to tell the truth or speak about it. Even those who worked in low paid jobs like cleaning or working in restaurants, refused to warn or educate their people about the true life they actually lived in Europe.

Although many Africans were living in these horrible conditions, still the numbers of people who were planning to travel to Europe increased, and there was nothing that could have changed their minds or convinced them otherwise. The obsession to travel became almost like rampant disease, and led many young Africans into the hands of conscienceless human traffickers who promised them "Heaven on Earth" when they were really walking into doom.

This was the case for my mother. Her story left me heartbroken as she began to share her painful experiences with her Madame.

She said, "My son, I didn't know this was how it was going to be! Since your father passed away, I have been struggling with three children, not having anyone to help me with financial support. I could barely afford clothes and food for myself and for my children. My son, do you know the hardship in our country Nigeria?"

I replied, nodding.

She continued: "Our leaders are very corrupt and they did nothing to help the poor. My son, it was a very hard life for me back then. I saw people in my village travelling out of the country, so I met with this lady who promised me that she would help me to travel to Europe and find me a job in a shoe factory. I saw many who travel come back to build big houses for their families and drive expensive cars. So I agreed, hoping that it would take us out of poverty. My Madame paid for everything, from my travel expenses to the clothes and the shoes I wore on the day I left."

She continued: "My son, hum… I was thankful that she picked me amongst the other girls in the village. When I arrived, she told me that I was to stand by the roadside and wait for the person to drive me to the shoe factory. Little did I know I was becoming a prostitute, working as a sex slave! My son, I was terrified and scared with my first encounter, it was as if God had forsaken our people in the condition we were in."

She wept, "Hum… I looked to my left, and there were all African girls from Ghana, Liberia, Congo, and Zimbabwe. And to my right, Nigerian, Sierra Leone, Gambia; the lists went on. When I sat down to talk to them, we all shared the same story. Some of them died after they contracted deadly diseases. But despite the losses, I still had to stay in the street, in order to pay back the money I owe to my Madame.

"I was charged 35,000.000 Italian Lira, and unless I completed the payment, I couldn't send any money back home to my family. My Madame had made me swear an oath that she would kill me if I were to disobey her. And if I reported her to the police, I would be poisoned and dissolved in acid, and my family would never see me again.

"My son… it was like slavery what Africans were doing to other Africans. Some that couldn't pay were found dead and their corpse missing. I was frightened and scared that if I refused to work, I might not see my children again. It was only after I finished my payment that I was allowed to come home to visit my family."

I asked, "What happened in the room when you visited that lady, that day that left you feeling sad?"

She replied, "Well... My son, after my payment, she demanded I pay an extra 5000 US dollars to finalize my release from the oath I had sworn to her. So I did, for the sake of my children."

Every evening when I turned on the television to watch the news, there was footage of black people piled into a boat arriving on the shores of Lampedusa, fleeing from their roots to Europe, not knowing what was ahead of them. This inspired me to visit sheltered accommodation that was provided for illegal immigrants. I then realized that 99% of them had similar stories of different expectations of how they imagined Europe; but going back wasn't an option. I began to see the similarities in the problems and the struggle that many were facing. They had to live through the hardship in order to prove to their families that their journey was a "success story".

So many Africans bought into the idea of "making it big" in Europe, but as a result many found themselves committing crimes and engaging in various activities to look "successful" in the eyes of their friends and family back home.

Those who couldn't make it big were scared to return home as they had nothing to fall back on. They feared being laughed at by their peers, so this explains why so many were left stranded in every street of Europe and the Western world.

It occurred to me that for some, their interest in coming to Europe was no longer for survival or for better conditions, but for their pride and ego. And it reinforces the perception that when you live and study in Europe, you are regarded as "better" than those who couldn't make it.

I always wondered why the African communities tolerated such perception, particularly as it caused hatred and division amongst our people.

# JOURNEY TO PAN-AFRICANISM

The need of many Africans coming to Europe was no longer a struggle for economical gain. It had become mandatory for self-recognition between many African bourgeoisies who were seeking validation and didn't feel that they had accomplished anything until they had European acronyms attached to their names and success. Many were caught up in the race to become the first black in a European institution or the first anything, as long as it didn't associate them with their roots.

This idea to seek for instant recognition made many African leaders appeal more to their European ambitions. It was embarrassing to watch the leaders of other nations working inward for their self-development and nation-building, while the African leaders were seeking an outward quick fix and instant gratification from their formal colonial masters, sacrificing the interests of their citizens for the benefit of few. For example, a Chinese leader would do everything to ensure the Chinese achieved an inner pride of the greatness of his nation. But as an African, there was nothing for me to be proud of about my history or my origins. I only had sad memories of my childhood and the poor surroundings. And the more I engaged with the European culture, the less proud I felt about my country and myself.

Though I tried to uplift myself from the hostility and the racism that was affecting blacks in Italy, the more I challenged racism the more I realized that as a black man I had nothing to offer or to compete with in argument. There was nothing I could say to convince a racist otherwise about my history; I could only react to the moral condemnation of not being treated fairly.

The pleasure of living in Europe became like a sedative to endure the pain of racism in exchange for instant comfort in a land far away from our home. So, it became a no-brainer to quickly cling onto a temporary solution to ease the pain and struggle of not having to go back to our roots and build and create opportunities for ourselves. The lack of vision and the courage to struggle and fight for our future made us failures to begin with; the thought of immediate reward was preventing blacks from focusing on finding a solution to the problems in their own countries.

All these things were happening to us because those who had been elected as leaders, governors, and community speakers, were continuously making bad choices that put the future of the next generation at risk. The few at the top that we had entrusted our future with were overly drunk by power and greed, and didn't even know the role they played in the world affairs of business, agriculture, science, and technology.

Africans today are scattered around the world with no sense of direction; they are physically active but mentally dead. Most have been brainwashed by the media, who are responsible for creating this false illusion of Europe as "Heaven on Earth" and maintaining Europe's dominant power over Africa. At the same time, they have promoted Africa in Europe as a jungle full of savages, which has made even blacks scared of returning to their own countries. I always wonder why the Africans couldn't reverse it.

What has made it even harder is that many Africans would rather engage with things which distract them daily than contribute to their development.

As an African, I wasn't educated about the African-American history, except for the stories my grandmother told me about slavery when I was growing up in Nigeria. The Transatlantic slave trade affected both Africans and Africans in America, and left them distorted, broken, and forgotten. However, many Africans, including myself, didn't see African-Americans as part of Africa. They were a group who were separated from us by language and culture, and the only thing we had in common was our skin color. There were certainly no acknowledgements of the African-American struggle within our African history.

I certainly never felt connected and related to the African-American struggles until my first encounter with an African-American, which was an experience I will never forget for the rest of my life. I have never met any black man so proud and happy to be African like Sergeant Shawn Bridges.

It was a sunny afternoon, at the festival Arena located in the city ground of Verona, Italy. Underground was the bus station where I was sitting, waiting to catch the last bus when a friend introduced me to Shawn Bridges, who was serving in the US Army based in Vicenza. He was about six feet tall, dark skinned, and I think he might have been in his early thirties, with a tattoo on his right arm.

Shawn had driven from Vicenza to attend the summer festival in the city where I was living at the time. He claimed to be an African-American who had transferred to Europe to serve for four years in the US military. At first, I didn't believe him until he showed his ID, then we sat down to talk.

I felt uncomfortable as an African without any knowledge about my history. And it was fascinating how much Shawn knew about slavery and African history; it left me speechless!

Shawn talked about his parents, and being raised by a single mother with six children while the father was in jail. He had joined the military to escape street life, as it was his only way out of prison and gang culture. I was surprised to hear about his upbringing, which was similar to mine when I was growing up in Nigeria.

I noticed he mentioned racism, so I asked, "Is there racism in America?"

He replied, "Of course! There is racism everywhere."

He explained that history had been "whitened" in the white man's history books, and that the black man had been "brainwashed" for hundreds of years, then went on, "The original man was black, in the continent called Africa, where the human race had emerged on the planet Earth.

"The black man, original man, built great empires and civilizations and cultures, while the white man was still living on al- fours in caves. 'The devil white man', down through history, out of his devilish nature had pillaged, murdered, raped, and exploited every race of man not white.

Human history's greatest crime was the traffic in black flesh when the devil white man went into Africa and murdered and kidnapped to bring to the West in chains, in slave ships, millions of black men, women and children, who were worked and beaten and tortured as slaves.

The devil white man cut these black people off from all knowledge of their own kind, and cut them off from any knowledge of their own language, religion, and past culture, until the black man in America was the earth's only race of people who had absolutely no knowledge of his true identity."[1]

I looked at him and I laughed!

But he continued, "In one generation, the black slave women in America had been raped by the slavemaster white man until there had begun to emerge a homemade, handmade, brainwashed race that was no longer even of its true color, that no longer even knew its true family names. The slavemaster forced his family name upon this rape-mixed race, which the slave master began to call 'the Negro'.

"This 'Negro' was taught of his native Africa that it was peopled by heathen, black savages, swinging like monkeys from trees. This 'Negro' accepted this, along with every other teaching of the slavemaster that was designed to make him accept and obey and worship the white man. And where the religion of every other people on earth taught its believers of a God with whom they could identify – a God who at least looked like one of their own kind – the slave master injected his Christian religion into this 'Negro'. This 'Negro' was taught to worship an alien God having the same blond hair, pale skin, and blue eyes as the slavemaster.

This religion taught the 'Negro' that black was a curse. It taught him to hate everything black, including himself. It taught him that everything white was good, to be admired, respected, and loved.

"It brainwashed this 'Negro' to think he was superior if his complexion showed more of the white pollution of the slavemaster. This white man's Christian religion further deceived and brainwashed this 'Negro' to always turn the other cheek, and grin, and scrape, and bow, and be humble, and to sing, and to pray, and to take whatever was dished out by the devilish white man, and to look for his pie in the sky, and for his heaven in the hereafter, while right here on earth the slavemaster white man enjoyed his heaven."[2]

At first, I thought he had issues with the white men, but the other part of me at that point was certain that I wasn't the only one seeking out the truth about our people. I was curious to find out how he knew all that information and why we weren't taught about that back in schools in Africa.

I didn't know much about African-American history, but everything he said seemed true and profound.

So I asked, "Can you show me proof?"

"Wait here!" he said, and he walked to his car to get a book. "Take this book. This is *Malcolm X*, it's the proof for you."

I went home that day feeling excited to have met someone like Shawn Bridges. I kept thinking about everything he'd said, the amount of knowledge he had about his people, and how proud he was of being a black man, so I was looking forward to read the book.

I woke up early the next morning before my mother left for work, and told her about the conversation I'd had with Shawn Bridges. I was eager to share with her what Shawn had said about the African-American struggle and how the white men had rewritten the black people's history.

But she immediately and angrily interrupted me. "African-American who? Who are they?" she snapped. "Son, be careful with the African-Americans, they are not part of us, nor do they belong to Africa!"

I didn't understand the hatred between the Africans and the African-Americans; I was only eager to know my history. So I didn't say a word, but would often sneak out of the house to read Malcolm X in the basement; his religious teachings and ideologies opened my eyes to a lot of the things I didn't know about our people, and reminded me of the stories my grandmother told me about the first arrival of the Europeans in Africa. The more I read about his teachings, the more I understood the problems that we were facing in our communities.

I didn't experience the struggle of the African-Americans who were under the white oppression, fighting for their rights to live as humans and to be treated as equal. But I will never forget how shocked I was when I began reading about the total horror of slavery. It made such an impact upon me that later it became one of my favorite subjects to talk about.[3] Malcolm X opened my eyes to the pain, struggle, and the ghetto conditions that the African-Americans were living under, and made me believe what Shawn had said about the white man.

The idea to unite amongst us under the umbrella of Pan-Africanism would have benefited blacks all over the world. This is something that Malcolm X first described in his visit to Nigeria, when he spoke at the Ibadan University's Trenchard Hall.

*"I urged that Africa's independent nations needed to see the necessity of helping to bring the Afro-American's case before the United Nations. I said that just as the American Jew is in political, economic, and cultural harmony with world Jewry, I was convinced that it was time for all Afro-Americans to join the world's Pan-Africanists. I said that physically we Afro-Americans might remain in America, fighting for our constitutional rights, but that philosophically and culturally we Afro-Americans badly needed to 'return' to Africa- and to develop a working unity in the framework of Pan Africanism."* [4]

By then I was convinced that Pan-Africanism was the only solution to the racial epidemic that had been inflicted upon us.

Pan-Africanism was based on the belief that African peoples, both on the continent and in the diaspora, share not merely a common history but a common destiny, which asserts that the fate of all African peoples and countries are intertwined. The ideology was a worldwide movement that aimed to 'unify and uplift', to encourage and strengthen bonds of solidarity between all people of African descent.

I began to research Black Nationalism and Pan-Africanist leaders like Patrice Lumumba, Thomas Sankara, Kwame Nkrumah, and many more. Pan-Africanism had a great significance, as it was an important step towards the end of the colonial powers in Africa, and it involved people from the Africans in the diaspora, including

Afro-Caribbean and African-Americans. The significance of the Pan-African movement urged for self-rule, and to resolve the problems faced in the African communities.

Dr. Nkrumah delivered a speech in 1961: (I Speak of Freedom).

*"Africa could become one of the greatest forces for good in the world. Africa is a land of 'vast riches' with mineral resources that 'range from gold and diamonds to uranium and petroleum'. The reason Africa isn't thriving was because the European powers have been taking all the wealth to themselves. If Africa could be independent of European rule then it could truly flourish and contribute positively to the world."* [5]

Although Pan-Africanism was the only solution to the black struggle, it had a lot of problems within the organization. Too many black leaders failed to accomplish the goal due to the lack of trust and jealousy. As Malcolm X pointed out: *"...too many organizations had been destroyed by leaders who tried to benefit personally. That because of jealousy and narrow-mindedness an order was given against him."*

He also made this statement before his assassination:

*"Black men are watching every move I make, awaiting their chance to kill me. I know, too, that I could suddenly die at the hands of some Negro hired by the white man. Or it could be some brainwashed Negro acting on his own idea that by eliminating me he would be helping out the white man, because I talk about the white man the way I do."*

I began to question, that though racism was the problem, why was there a driving force of hatred, envy, and jealousy within the black organization? That had led to the assassination of some of the greatest leaders, like Patrice Lumumba, and many others who were betrayed by their own people.

I was saddened to see that there was a problem deeper within our roots, which was beneath the surface of racism. Many blacks were suffering across the globe, but as a group they couldn't stick together to tackle their common issue!

After reading in Malcolm X's book of his attempts to free the mind of many African-Americans, and his assassination, I suddenly lost faith in Pan-Africanism and began to question the Black Intelligence as a whole.

- Why would our people allow the assassination of some of our greatest leaders?
- Why was Malcolm X killed?
- Why did every leader who tried to wake us and help us to restore our pride of being African, end up being killed by our own people?

These facts made me question the older generation who "supposedly" had more wisdom than I had, but showed a lack of interest in this type of conversation and ridiculed my efforts to discover why blacks were acting and behaving in this way. Some of them found it amusing and laughed at what I was trying to achieve. It was frustrating how our people would openly glorify ignorance instead of reasoning. These pathological behaviors were almost unbearable and impossible to challenge.

The older generation, who I believed to have gained more wisdom and knowledge through their life experiences, were carrying these same behavioral traits, which impaired young ones from questioning it. One thing I noticed about blacks is that they don't like anything around them that looks or acts differently. They want everybody to be just the same. That fear of change had cost the lives of many of our great leaders who have tried to bring changes into the lives of our people.

As Malcolm X said: *"I know that societies often have killed the people who have helped to change those societies."* This fear of change and refusal of blacks to take orders from another black keeps the whole race on a lower level. And these weaknesses were mainly used against them by the Europeans, who have always used this as a means of dealing with the so-called weaker races of the world. We could have deprived them of control over us if we were united in our struggle, but the lack of trust and jealousy within our race made us act as subordinated to the European 'superior race'. This example also applied in the slave plantation: *How was one white man able to maintain himself on a plantation where there were thirty or forty slaves?* [6]

These divide-and-conquer rules only work on people with a lower morale and sense of values; in most cases, it works effectively amongst the black race. Jews put first their race, no matter whether the Jew is a doctor, merchant, housewife, or student. Whatever the profession, first and foremost he, or she, thinks Jew.[7] This greater readiness to subordinate purely personal interests, makes it easier to establish comprehensive communities. This state of mind, which subordinates the interests of the ego to the conservation of the community, is really the first premise for every truly human culture. In giving one's own life for the existence of the community lies the crown of all sense of sacrifice. [8]

Blacks have always slavishly followed leadership, but unfortunately sometimes those leaders were selected for them by the traducer of the race. In most cases, the enemies of the race will find a "puppet" leader willing to do anything they want accomplished, and will finance him and give him sufficient publicity before the world. Too often, blacks refuse to willingly follow a leader with a constructive program, which results in them choosing the wrong kind of leader most of the time. Inasmuch as they have failed to exercise foresight, however, those who have deceived them gain immediate attention by making trivial remarks and exciting appeal even when they don't seem to care about them. [9]

These "puppet" leaders that fight to defend their European interests are mostly the ones who get elected to govern over the rest, who don't understand why they remain poor despite the wealth and the resources of their country, and fail to hold these leaders accountable for their wrong-doings. Yet blacks have forgotten the men who have served their own advantages, and praise the heroes who have renounced their own happiness. [10]

These black leaders are typically those with Ph.D. and Doctorate degrees from some of the most prestigious colleges and universities, but they have failed to apply any of their education to further themselves and their race as the white man does.[11] They are only good at spending their country's wealth on the white man's luxurious cars, clothes, and hotels around the world, and patronizing the white and Asian inventions, while the average citizen can barely feed themselves or afford such a luxurious lifestyle. This is because the black leader is so brainwashed in seeing himself as better than or different from the rest of his people, that he begins to separate himself from their struggle.

Instead, they should be focusing their every effort towards building a nation and creating opportunities for its people as other ethnic groups have done.[12] As an example, in every black community the majority of businesses and commercial products are owned and produced by people who are of other races and ethnicity. So, every night the owners of those businesses go home with that black community's money, which helps the black communities to stay poor.[13]

The black race can never become independent and recognized as human beings who are truly equal with other human beings, until they start doing for themselves what others are doing for their kind. By letting the black people, wherever and however possible, patronize and hire their own kind, they will be building up the black race's ability to manage for itself. Only in this way will the black race be respected!

The number one thing the white man can never give a black man is self-respect![14] Every black man must step out of his kingdom in his head, and start seeing the bigger picture for his race, community, and nation; only then will a real attitude for change begin. He who wants to act alone, could act destructively and in no way could he organize. For the innermost essence of all communities requires that the individual renounces putting forward his personal opinion and interests, and sacrifices both in favor of a larger group.[15]

But this won't happen until the black man changes his point of view and begins constructing a program that will bring him out of the wilderness of self-destruction[16]. From this alone, we can understand how many are able to bear up faithfully in a life which imposes on them nothing but poverty and frugality, yet gives the community the foundation of its existence.[17] Development requires willingness on the part of the individual to sacrifice himself for the community, and not the sickly imaginings of cowardly know-it-alls and critics.[18]

The biggest challenge that is facing almost every black man and woman today is the problem of SELF-PRESERVATION.

For example, in the most primitive living creatures, the instinct of self-preservation does not go beyond concern for their own ego. Egoism, as we designate this urge, goes so far that it even embraces time; the moment itself claims everything, granting nothing to the coming hours. In this condition, the individual lives only for himself, seeks food only for his present hunger, and fights only for his own life. Even community between male and female, beyond pure mating, demands an extension of the instinct of self-preservation, since concern and struggle for the ego are now directed towards the second party; the male sometimes seeks food for the female, but for the most part both seek nourishment for the young. Nearly always, one comes to the defense of the other, and this is the first, though infinitely simple, form of a sense of sacrifice. As soon as this sense extends beyond the narrow limits of the family, the basis for the formation of larger organisms and finally formal states is created. In the lowest people of the earth, this quality is present only to a very slight extent, so that often they do not go beyond the formation of the family. The greater the readiness to subordinate purely personal interests, the higher is raised the ability to establish comprehensive communities. [19]

In order to execute a constructive program that could solve the everyday black problem, we would need the whole of the communities to be concentrated on this, so that every single individual could become inwardly conscious of the importance of this struggle and exclude all other problems of the day, which might have a distracting effect. Also, it would have to be understood that future generations of our people depended on its solution.

After several years in Italy, due to lack of jobs during the global economic downturn, I relocated to the Netherlands. Living in Amsterdam, I noticed that there were different groups of blacks that originally came from other continents, but from Dutch colonies. The Surinamese and those from the Netherlands Antilles were friendly people and warm to be around, but they had the same behavior as the Africans and acted as if they were from Africa, even though they were of Dutch nationality. They also faced similar problems of discrimination and racism. And they had similar traits and behavioral issues among themselves, like violence, fighting, selling drugs, and illegal activity. Although the Netherlands was known as the only country in Europe where drugs like marijuana were legal, some of these groups still chose to sell it on the street corners.

After several months of living and working with them, I never really understood their culture. But as an African from the motherland, I could tell that parts of their culture and traits had similarities to mine. It was as if their culture was taken from us Africans, but that they were Caribbean. Drugs, crime, and violence were inevitable among these groups, in the same way as I had witnessed within our people from the sub-Saharan Africa. Once again, I realized that blacks weren't ready to confront these behavioral dilemmas, as if these things weren't important to them.

I spend a lot of time trying to integrate into the Dutch system, like trying to understand the Dutch culture and learn the language by attending evening school after long a day of work. After nine months of trying, I found myself losing passion to learn the language, so I decided to relocate to the United Kingdom.

The United Kingdom was the right choice for me, as in England I didn't have to learn a new language, thanks to my colonial background. As far as I am concerned, the English language was the only thing that united many tribes and cultures in my home country Nigeria.

# STUDY AND OBSERVATION

L iving in the United Kingdom was a great opportunity for me; I thought I knew the English language so well, thanks to my postcolonial country, but soon realized that the average Englishman couldn't understand the language I spoke. Some of them complained, while others completely refused to have a conversation with me due to my "African" accent!

One thing I enjoyed most about England was that they promoted equal rights, although racism was still present in their society. England was a multicultural society that recognized the value and dignity of all races and ethnicities. There were a lot of people from different countries and cultural backgrounds derived from its colonial influences around the world. The citizens of those countries had been drawn to England because of its policies for human rights.

I developed a good relationship with the Afro-Caribbeans, who were mostly from Jamaica and Guyana nationalities. These groups were best known for their annual Notting Hill Carnival, which is regarded as the largest street festival in Europe. I enjoyed attending the carnival to celebrate their culture and to taste some of their best cuisine. I perceived the British Afro-Caribbean culture as being similar to other cultures I had encountered in Italy and Netherland.

As time went by, however, I noticed the same problem of violence and hatred among these groups. Despite the fact that they were nice people with an open culture, they also had numerous problems. Young people from African and Caribbean descent were often involved in knife crimes that took the lives of many of their own.

These behavioral traits within the Caribbean and African communities in the United Kingdom, were the same ones which Malcolm X described in his book regarding the African-Americans and which Shawn Bridges had spoken of.

No matter where I went geographically, I noticed these behaviors among the black people. It seemed that there was always jealousy and envy-related conflict. Although they were welcoming to almost every race, they were resentful toward their own. It was as if someone had "copy & pasted" the same behavior I had witnessed in my hometown in Nigeria.

The more I studied and observed the black culture and behavior, the more I discovered that there was something beyond the racial barrier and discrimination that was preventing blacks from accomplishing what other races have achieved. This unharmonious behavior was creating a dysfunctional culture within them. For some reason, the Ghanaians hated the Nigerians, the Surinamese couldn't stand those from the Dutch Antilles, and the Jamaicans didn't like the Guyanese.

This was also witnessed by Samuel, an African-American who travelled across the world to serve as a missionary in Africa, but discovered that the Africans never cared about the African-Americans. He wrote: *"The Africans never asked us to come. The Africans don't even see us; they don't even recognize us as the brothers and sisters they sold, we try every way we can to show them love but they reject us. They never even listen to how we've suffered. And if they listen, they say stupid things like why don't you speak our language? Why can't you remember the old ways and why aren't you happy in America, if everyone there drives motorcars?"*[1]

The sense of strong unity within families and communities that was easily seen in other racial groups, was lacking in the black communities; it seemed that there was a natural instinct of hatred within them.

A black man was less likely to humble himself to another black man without a reward or financial gain, so he refused to be loyal and respectful to his fellow man. Such behavior was a blueprint in the black community; for some reason, every black man lived in his own kingdom. This mindset was carried around in his community, places of worship, schools, clubs, and work places. This behavior was like a virus that affected every fabric in the black community; the more dysfunctional it became, the harder it was for them to stay united.

Yet these behaviors were never questioned or challenged. A black man would kill another black man to protect his 'status'. This 'Big Man Syndrome'[2] made it impossible to hold anyone accountable, and made the black communities and nations physically and culturally isolated from the rest of the world.

Behavior that was regarded as pathological anywhere else was considered routine, and often glamorized. In most neighborhoods, stores were boarded up, windows were broken, nothing seemed to work, and many people seem to have nothing to do. Many areas seemed to have lost all institutions, except the churches, the liquor store, and the gas station. The streets were irrigated with alcohol, urine, and blood. Violence was a normal part of daily existence, to the point that it was no longer a surprise to witness a knife crime or hear the sound of gunfire in the street, at parties or clubs. The streets became like war zones, governed by young gangs who had lost their innocence at an early age and been initiated into a culture of hardened street attitudes, slang expressions, flamboyant rituals, and ghetto lifestyle. Mothers regularly saw their sons arrested and taken to prison. Drugs and alcohol addiction reached epidemic proportions, due to high level of unemployment.[3]

I dedicated many years to studying African history and civil rights leaders across the United States and the Caribbean.

Many civil rights leaders wrote about the challenges facing people of color in the Western world in the early 60s. These great men and women, who were born into the struggle at that time, dedicated their entire lives to regain the "Black Pride" during the days of racial turmoil in North America. They were fighting to end segregation, but as a race, they failed to recognize and acknowledge the pathological behavior that was found among the black culture.

As Frederick Douglas said in 1852, *"It is vain that we talk of being men, if we don't work of men"*.

These similarities in behavior were identical to those in Sub-Sahara Africa, in Europe, and the Caribbean despite the geographical differences.

I realized that many black people tend to lack the ability to become valuable and efficient within their communities, society, and race. Often, I sat wondering why blacks couldn't do for themselves what other races had done in terms of nation-building. Even the so-called "educated blacks" who studied in Western universities like Harvard, Yale, Columbia, and Oxford, did not have this point of view, or understand the need to build his own nation and industry. They failed to realize that by imitating what others were doing, nothing new had been accomplished, and in their efforts to imitate the white mans they showed no mental power to understand what was best for their own people. Thereby, the "unusual gifts" of the race have not been developed, and the world continues to wonder, what is the black man good for?[4] And why is Africa still in a backward state?

For example, a Frenchman is not brought up to be objective among the French people; his extreme emphasis is on the greatness of France in all the fields of culture or, as the Frenchman puts it, of 'civilization'. [5] On the other hand, when the black man he finishes his education, he is either Americanized or Europeanized[6] in his way of thinking, since he has been taught to act European. Therefore, he finds nothing interesting about himself and becomes a hopeless liability to his race. [7]

Our "educated elites" read enormously, book for book, letter for letter, yet I would not describe them as 'well-read'. True, they possess a mass of 'knowledge', but their brain is unable to organize and register the material they have taken in. They lack the art of sifting out what is valuable for them in a book from that which is not worth retaining.

Reading is no end in itself, but a means to an end. It should primarily help to fill the framework constituted by every man's talents and abilities. In addition, it should provide the tools and building materials which the individual needs for his life's work, regardless of whether this is a primitive struggle for sustenance or the satisfaction of a high calling. It should also transmit a general world view.

In all cases, however, it is essential that the content of what one reads at any time should not be transmitted to the memory in the sequence of the book or books. Like the stone of a mosaic, it should fit into the general world picture in its proper place, and thus help to form this picture in the mind of the reader. Otherwise, a confused muddle of memorized facts arises, which are only worthless. Such a reader now believes himself in all seriousness to be 'educated', to understand something of life and to have knowledge, while in reality, with every new acquisition of this kind of 'education', he is growing more and more detached from the world.[8] This pathology is common among some African political leaders; they lack the systematic effort to make a long-term goal, which in time has undermined Africa's potential.

During the colonial period, the British "acknowledged" that after their withdrawal, the Chiefs and Kings would inherit power, since it had been disinherited from them in the past. Before the independence, the "educated elite" who grazed in the learned pastures of London's law schools, came home with the conviction that after British withdrawal, power could not be entrusted to 'Chiefs and Kings', but should be in the hands of the literate and civilized men who understood constitutional law and practice. However, they self-selected themselves as the people who should substitute and steer the right course of the nation, due to their sophisticated wisdom and educational advantages.

After independence, the "Chiefs and Kings" found it deeply offensive, and obviously perverse, that power was given to the "Modernizers". They argued that the "Modernizers" were bound to make a mess of it. The "Chiefs and Kings" had plenty of experience, thought they admitted that their forms of government might need to be modernized, their institutions reformed, and their powers redefined.[9] They were eager for development and to assimilate the fruits of modernization, as long as it could be made digestible to improve historical customs.

On the other hand, the "Modernizers" stood on the ground of the European culture, as they understood it, with the conviction that African people would become civilized under the British or

European model. They believed that "civilization must come from abroad", [10] but this was no good to the Africans, because it was created in conformity to the needs of Europeans. The system might have made Africa free from its colonial power, but in terms of political and literate culture, Africa ceased to be Africa. [11]

These differences created a "state of chaos" and soon became war, on differences of ideology and issues of principle. The failure to develop and carry out a model of government that could suit the needs of African people automatically imprisoned the continent into a foreign system of government. The "educated elite" believed that "Modernization meant Modernization", and that if they did as the Europeans told them, their countries would be developed for them! [12] They never asked for ideas about whether the European model would be suitable, or whether any modification should be made, or whether any African practices or institutions could be associated with it. [13] They continued to wander in some no-man's-land of their own, waiting for the trumpet of destiny at some unthinkable time in the future, to swing wide the doors of civilization and let them in.[14]

For example, after the Japanese resurgence with defeat of Russia in the war of 1904, Japan had remained independent and resisted being subjected to the imposition of a totally external culture. Japan was able to look to the West to whatever might be useful, while rejecting what was not useful.[15] Japan today has copied from the First World countries until they were on par and even overtook some First World countries in certain industries.

Other Asian nations, in many cases, started off equal or lower in GDP per capita when compared with a number of African countries. In 1957, Ghana and South Korea had about the same GDP per capita; South Korea had no mineral wealth, instead what they had was national systems of innovation, and critically, they invested in human capital. South Korea had a "national leadership" focused on rapid economic development, while Ghana had no program of similar nature on record. Yet no African leader has pursued a single-minded determination towards the improvement of the lives of its citizens.

Today, the black leaders have been so busy doing what they are told to do that they have not stopped long enough to think about the meaning of these things. They have borrowed the ideas of the Europeans instead of delving into things and working out some thought of their own.[16] With respect to development, no man knows what he can do or achieve until he tries! The African leaders have lost ground in recent years for not being able to do for themselves what others have done for themselves, like the United Arab Emirates (UAE) and Asia in term of development.

In observing African politics, I realized that every nation requires five stages towards development:

## 1. Philosophical Stages

This stage requires mostly philosophers, thinkers, and visionaries to create the ideal state. This requires the ruler (kings or elites) to have an idea, direction, and to foresee a future for his nation which the people must uphold. An idea or philosophy that is sold to common people can only hope for victory if the people adhere to the new doctrine and declare their readiness to undertake the necessary struggle. It has to be understood that "a man does not die for a business, but only for ideas". [17]

## 2. Development Stages

This stage requires the ruler to make the necessary decisions to maximize his ideas or philosophy. This stage begins with national and cultural identity and increasing urbanization like the creation and the mapping of the city, towns, houses, roads, railways, and airport. This should be followed by "agricultural revolution", but it should be acknowledged that nature knows no political boundaries, nature does not reserve the soil for the future possession of any particular nation or race. On the contrary, the soil exists for the people who possess the force to take it and the industry to cultivate it.[18] The country must invest in industrialization, technological breakthrough, science, welfare, and the military. And there must be improvements in health services and social infrastructure (like schools, universities, hospitals). The people should also be taught a common language so that they can better communicate with the government and access public services.

## 3. Freedom Stages

This stage requires the cleansing of the culture to be extended to nearly all fields. Theater, art, literature, cinema, entertainment, the press, posters, and window displays must be cleansed of all manifestations of the rotting world, and placed in the service of moral, political, and cultural idea. Public life must be freed from the stifling perfume of the modern eroticism, and just as freed from all unmanly prudish hypocrisy. In all these things, the goal and the road must be determined by concern for the preservation of the health of the people's mind, body, and soul.[19] This stage requires the ruler to practice citizens' rights, self-identity, freedom of speech, and political advancement.

## 4. Economic Stages

This stage requires the country to be economically independent and rely on its self-sufficiency. The country would be limited to the goods and services produced within its own borders, without foreign trade, because the economy needs to self-sustain to thrive. At this stage, international trading is prohibited as it is more costly than domestic trade. Doing this will reinforce the growth production of self-made products like food, clothes, and shelter. This will help the country to build a stronger economy and national pride.

## 5. Worldly Stages

This stage requires the country to compete globally in all areas: banking, government, policies, markets, laws, judicial system, and currency... Trading globally gives the country the opportunity to be exposed to new markets and products. Services can also be traded, like tourism and transportation. This stage helps the country to sell its ideology, promote cultural identity, and gain respect from other nations across the world.

There has never been a successful civilized nation which lacks these stages in their development. The current reality of Africa made me believe that African leaders have been busy doing the right thing in reverse from five to one! They have given up on their ability to create for themselves. As the African says: *'A white man wears a sock and jacket because it's cold in Europe, an African man wears a sock and jacket in Africa because the white man wore it!'*

There must be reasons for the general and continual failure of African countries; in spite of the "education" of some of our leaders, there is still a huge gap in the supply chain of thinkers and philosophers* who could point the continent in the right direction. Though Western democracy allowed decisions to be made by the majority vote of the people, this system has failed, and has proven not suitable for African people.

In the early years of Europe's development, countries like Britain, France, Russia, Germany, Italy, and many others, practiced nationalism, fascism, socialism, communism, and the constitutional monarchy form of government. They understood that in order for a nation to flourish, it must first come to its full realization, knowing its strengths and weaknesses. By acknowledging its potential, the nation can then adjust to a system of democracy. History suggests that it took the British and French over 150 years for their models to be produced, and this derived from a society already divided into established social classes. These models' effectiveness highly depended upon the hegemony of the widely-spread "middle strata" capable of dominating society and its economy, which many African countries don't yet have. [20]

It is fairly easy to understand that a new nation, emerging from colonial oppression, has to modernize their institution, their modes of government, and their political and economic structure. In the haste to adopt the new Western form of democracy, African leaders accepted a foreign model instead of building upon their own democratic tradition. So, the intelligent questions one must ask are, why adopt models from those very countries or systems that have oppressed and disposed you? [21] And why is Africa not able to build a model of its own that will suit the working class, who don't understand politics and the "power of vote" in a democratic process?

This Western multiparty system has become a means for the newly-elected leader to abuse power and use the state machinery to advance only the economic interests of his ethnic group and exclude the others. Virtually all Africa's tribal conflicts happened under democratic governments who have politically marginalized and excluded a certain group. One might have expected the "educated elite" to draw their attention to these issues, but instead they still choose to cling on to democracy, hoping that one day their nation will become 'modernized'. No people can go forward when the majority of those who should know better have chosen to go backwards.[22]

Some African leaders preach the principles of democracy, and the very next moment they barter it away for their personal gain. For instance, once these leaders formed their political parties, they set off on endless journeys to chase their voters – penetrating places they'd never been before, crossing rivers never before encountered, confronting languages never spoken before. And they succeeded by gaining moral support from the local enthusiasts[23] who had been influenced in the wrong way, with the help of a new car, bags of rice, foodstuffs, and money for bribery. In many African "democratic" governments, there has been a lack of trust between the people and the "beneficiary" leaders *(who do not occupy a job but simply occupy a wage).* [24]

As the years have gone by, the rich gap has widened – on one end, a great mass of resentful and impoverished people; on the other end, a small minority with the abundance of wealth.[25] In the need for Western aid to help with inadequate infrastructure and a high percentage of unemployment, many African countries seem to have been trapped and bamboozled into practicing 'democracy'. This only advantages Western exploitation, while Africa's poor people are yet to reap the benefit of their nations' wealth and resources.

As the Afro-beat legend Fela Kuti expresses in a song entitled, *Teacher Don't Teach Me Nonsense*:

>*Who is our teacher? Is Oyinbo (The white man)*
>*Who teach us dem-o-cr-azy?*
>*Oyinbo teach us*
>*Oyinbo for Europe*
>*Oyinbo teach us many things*
>*Me I no gree copy Oyinbo style*
>*(I don't agree to copy the white man style)*
>*Let us think say, Oyinbo know pass me*
>*(let assume the white are wiser)*
>*I come to think about this demo-crazy*

>DEMO-CRAZY
>*Crazy demo*
>*Demonstration of craze*
>*Crazy demonstration*
>*If it not craze*
>*Why for Africa?*
>*As time go*
>*Things just bad*
>*They bad more and more*
>*Poor man dey cry*
>*Rich man dey mess*
>*This is Demo-crazy*

*If good a teacher teach something*
*And student make mistake*
*Teacher must talk so*
*But Oyinbo don't talk so*
*Then they support and support them*
*That says that the teaching got meaning*
*Different different meaning*
*Different different kinds of meaning.*[26]

This explains the incompetence and the imbalance of some of the political behavior by African "leaders" under the current "democracy".

As the Russian President Vladimir Putin said, *"When an African becomes rich, his bank accounts are in Switzerland. He travels to France for medical treatment. He invests in Germany. He buys from Dubai. He consumes Chinese. He prays in Rome or Mecca. His children study in Europe. He travels to Canada, USA, and Europe for tourism. If he dies, he will be buried in his native country of Africa. Africa is just a cemetery for Africans. How could a cemetery be developed?"*

African people can't be shiftless and expect someone else to think and decide about their own affairs while they have the abilities to think for themselves. These behaviors have proved to other races that blacks lack the ability to think and act for themselves! They must take responsibility to create their own destiny and build their nation.

I noticed the same pathology among some blacks in the West with regard to racism and discrimination. They tend to complain about racial problems and blame racism for why blacks are under-performing. The more I studied the black behavior in the West, the more I realized that there are three types of black men.

An educated white man – an observer said recently – differs from the educated black man, who so readily forsakes the elements of his race. When a white man sees persons of his own race tending downward to a level of disgrace, he does not rest until he works out some plan to lift such unfortunates to higher ground. But the black man forgets the delinquents of his race, and goes his own way to feather his own nest.[27] As everywhere, in every struggle, there are always: the Fighters, the Lukewarm, and the Traitors.[28]

## 1. The Traitors

These are mainly the "upper class" that are always busy trying to impress the white man with their social status, while ignoring the struggle of their own race; they are the gatekeepers who have betrayed the loyalty and the needs of their people for shameless private advantages. This group believes that they have the divine power to speak on race-related issues on behalf of other blacks; they suppress the race by reaffirming that racism is the primary reason why blacks cannot achieve what other races, like Hispanic, Asian, and Middle Easterners, have achieved. Although they speak of racism and discrimination, they only use this as a tactic to keep the rest of blacks at bay while securing their position and enriching themselves. Mostly, they are the ones who strive to become the "first black" in every white institution or establishment. These "racial racketeers" are found on the Forbes List and in the leadership positions like politicians, [29] ministers, and directors of community centers, media, and enterprises that affect the life and the future of other black people.

## 2. The Lukewarm

These are the back-up singers to the Traitors. These groups are hardly interested in any project that will advance their race. They always sit on the fence, not knowing where they fit or where they belong in the black struggle. They speak only when it is convenient and when there is something to gain. They are the biggest threat and the most dangerous among the groups. They are responsible for carrying out the orders or the dirty jobs that the external forces want accomplished in their communities. They operate as spies in black meetings, government, and institutions. They are willing to work to advance the oppression of their race as long as there is a financial reward.

## 3. The Fighters

These are good leaders and role models in their various ways within their communities. They are the real servants of the people who live among them, think with them, feel for them, and die for them. They believe in constructive programs that could help improve the lives of their people. Mostly, these groups have little opportunity or chance of making it to the top of ladder like the first group. They are mostly silenced for speaking the meaningful truth that the first and the second groups don't want to hear or fail to acknowledge. These groups have the best interests of their people at heart, and sacrifice their time for the betterment of others rather than extracting from them.

These Fighters must hold the position of leadership and decision-making and the people must love, support, and protect them by any means necessary from the first and second groups, who compromise the future of the people. This group must be the one with which we must entrust our future; only a sheep will stand aside and watch a wolf kill one of his own. So, we must stand together to protect those who are dear to us, and support them until they can outnumber the first and the second groups.

We must not accept any internal or external forces taking out those who put their lives on the line to secure the future of our people. We must not allow the enemies to take out the leaders who are fighting for our struggle, otherwise it will be a "Divine Curse" upon us as a race.

We must not let history repeat itself in the case of our fallen leaders in the past, like Marcus Garvey, Malcolm X, Thomas Shakara, Martin Luther King Jr, Patrice Lumumba, and many others.

We must choose our leaders from this group, who appear to be most likely to devote their lives in doing what they judge to be in the interest of the community, and who are never prepared to act against it. They are the men for our purpose. However, a close watch must be kept on them at all times, to see if they stick to the principles under the external influence or money. They must always do what is best for the community.[30] From a political standpoint, there is nothing more dangerous for a country or communities than to be led by jacks-of-all-trades who know everything but cannot achieve anything!

Many men and women who hold positions of power choose corruption over good governance that serves the needs of their people. For example, a law enforcement officer who is willing to accept bribery instead of enforcing the law of the land.

It would be the most dreadful disgrace for a shepherd to keep sheep-dogs so badly bred and trained that disobedience, hunger, or some other bad trait led them to worry the sheep and behave more like wolves than dogs. We must therefore take every possible precaution to prevent our leaders treating our people like that because of their superior strength, and behaving like savage tyrants.[31]

If we can prevent this pathology within the whole community, then we are most likely to find justice in such a community. Similarly, injustice is prevalent in a really badly-run community. We must therefore construct what we think is a happy community by securing the happiness not of a select minority, but of the whole.[32] We have the ability to decide and to act on our decisions however much effort is needed.[33]

In observing the black struggle, I then – and even more in the years to come – arrived at the following conviction: as people we have not been educated to understand what is best for us. Often our parents or guardians do not see or create possibilities for the younger generation; they are reactive rather than proactive; and most of the time they fail to share knowledge or information that could transform or prevent the new generation from repeating previous mistakes. So the youth have to figure life out for themselves, which in many times slows down their growth!

For example: in a basement apartment, consisting of two stuffy rooms, dwells a worker's family of seven. Among the five children, there is a boy of, let us assume, three years old. This is an age in which the first impressions are made on the consciousness of the child. Talented people retain traces of memory from this period to advanced old age.

The very narrowness and overcrowding of the room do not lead to favorable conditions, and quarrelling and wrangling very frequently arise as a result. In these circumstances, people do not live with one another, they press against one another. Every argument here, even the most trifling – which in a spacious apartment can be reconciled by mild segregation, thus solving itself –leads to loathsome wrangling without end. Among the children, of course, this is still bearable. They always fight among themselves but quickly forget about it.

But if this battle is carried on between the parents themselves, then – if only very gradually – the results of such visual instruction must ultimately become apparent in the children. This mutual quarrel often takes the form of brutal attacks by the father against the mother, which may be hard to imagine for anyone who does not know this scene.

At the age of six, the pitiable little boy – now morally poisoned and physically undernourished – goes off to public school. After a great struggle, he may learn to read and write, but that is about all. Doing any homework is out of the question. On the contrary, the mother and father, even in the presence of the children, talk about his teacher and school in terms which are not fit to be repeated, and they are more inclined to curse the teachers to their face than to take their little offspring across their knees and teach them some sense.

All the other things that the little fellow hears at home do not tend to increase his respect for his dear fellow men. When at the age of fourteen, the young man is discharged from school, it is hard to decide what is stronger in him: his incredible stupidity as far as any real knowledge and ability are concerned; or the corrosive insolence of his behavior, combined with an immorality.

This young man, to whom even now hardly anything is holy, has encountered no greatness, so what position can he pursue in the life into which he is now preparing to emerge?

The three-year-old child has become a fifteen-year-old despiser of all authority. This young man has seen nothing which might inspire him to anything higher.

But only now does he enter the real university of this existence. Now he begins the same life which he has seen his father living throughout his childhood years. He hangs around the street corners and bars, curses God and the world, and at length is convicted of some particular offence and sent to a house of correction. [34]

This behavior found among many black communities has kept the race in a "destructive state". Because anyone who rises by his own efforts from his previous position in life to a higher one, is seen as an upstart. Ultimately, this struggle, which is often so hard, kills all pity. His own painful struggle for existence destroys his feelings for the misery of those who have remained behind[35]. The man who is fighting for his own existence cannot have much left over for the community[36]. In this particular respect, his education is a failure and disastrous, because in its present predicament the race is especially in need of vision and invention to give humanity something new.

I am firmly convinced that basically, and on the whole, all creative ideas appear in our youth, insofar as any such are present. I distinguish between the wisdom of age – consisting solely of greater thoroughness and caution, due to the experience of a long life – and the genius of youth, which pours out thoughts and ideas with inexhaustible fertility. It is this youthful genius which provides the building materials and plans for the future, from which the older generation takes the stones, carves them, and completes the edifice.[37]

If we were to do the identical thing from generation to generation, acting from the instinct of self-preservation rather than from the preservation of the race and not letting go of the differences, we would not make any progress.

It may not be easy in the first generation, but we may succeed with the second or later generations, as long as we understand the pathology that has prevented the race from reaching its full greatness.

No culture can be said to be better or worse than any other. Cultures are just different, and we must learn to cherish their differences. All cultures are equally entitled to respect, and the standards for evaluating or criticizing a culture must come from within that culture itself! [38] The progress of a race is like climbing an endless ladder; it is impossible to climb higher without first taking a lower step. [39]

# CHANGE OF PERCEPTION

Every day, people are faced with choices, big or small, within their life, work, or communities. The more decisions they make, the more tired the brains get, leading them to either give less thought when making decisions or to choose a safe option simply to avoid the effort of making a difficult decision.

Everyone makes mistakes, but not everyone learns from it. A lot of black people tend to make the same mistakes over and over again, and fail to make any real progress but can't find out why. The only way for anyone to avoid repeating the same mistake is to fully acknowledge and embracing the errors. So many people would rather blame others for their mistake instead of admitting it themselves. When we make mistakes, it can be hard to admit them, because doing so feels like an attack on our self-worth. This tendency of denying and not admitting one's own mistakes can lead to bad decision-making. When you look across the Caribbean, the North American to Africa, blacks are facing exactly the same issues that previous generations dealt with, but are expecting different results.

Just like Albert Einstein said, insanity is doing the same thing over and over again and expecting different results.

Why is it that black communities and businesses failed to thrive as those of the Europeans and Asians? Is it simply that blacks cannot do as well as whites or Asians? Or it is because they lack the knowledge to run businesses and communities that can compete with whites or Asians? When other races see a problem, they do something about it, while blacks complain about it as if the problem can solve itself.

Some people can assert these behaviors to stereotype, but there must be a reason why the same behaviors keep reoccurring among the black race.

For example, in the United States of America, some African-Americans organize marches and protests against the injustice of police brutality. When that same "injustice" and violence happens within their own communities, no one tends to protest or acknowledge there is a problem. These same behaviors can also be traced to the Caribbean, and blacks in Africa.

One thing I learned from the "white devils" is their abilities of efficiency and pro-activeness, which is rarely found among the blacks! The ability for blacks to make the "Right Choice", in the right circumstances, at the right time, in the right place, is what has prevented the race from making a progressive step. From the impoverished conditions of Africa (which is a matter of choice of the government), to many African leaders who made no effort to understand the African-American struggle but benefit from the equal rights law which permitted some of them and their children to study or to sit in the white man's restaurants across North America. Or to the African-Americans that choose to look toward Egyptian history instead of focusing their efforts towards their places of origin in sub-Saharan Africa. Or to the average man who is unable to make a choice between getting a job or robbing his fellow man. Or to a single mother, who has multiple children with different men out of wedlock, jumping from one bad relationship to the next. In every situation, everything is a matter of the choices we make.

Many black scholars have been trying to solve the "Black Problem" for years. Many failed miserably, while others blame the white supremacy for the conditions and the struggle in which blacks find themselves. Throughout, though, none of them have been able to pinpoint exactly what the black problem is! Yet blacks who live in Africa, in the Caribbean, in North America, and across Europe, all complain of the same problem.

In order to solve this problem, we have to admit that the black problem is unique and the same no matter where they live geographically. Just as we can easily identify the rhythms and melodies of any black music, regardless of where it's found, the same applies to blacks' behavior, regardless of where they are located.

For us to understand the black problem, we cannot look elsewhere for the answers without first looking within. While a qualified medical professional wouldn't carry out a treatment without proper diagnosis of the patient, somehow, many black scholars, leaders, and activists, have fallen short in this area of "diagnosing" the black problem. Some actively defend to death that the white men and white supremacy are the cause of black suffering; yet others have a glimpse of hope that by fighting racism and white supremacy, they are actually solving the black problem. While blacks were focusing on fighting the white supremacy in their homeland and abroad, somehow they forgot to look within for a solution to the problem, and in the meantime other groups like Chinese, Indians, and Arabs, have evolved.

The more I studied the work of some of the great black writers like Carter G. Woodson and Dr. Ani Marimba, the more I wanted to understand why black people were so resentful towards their own progress. *It is because they hate change? Or are they too afraid to stand for what is right?* I asked myself. My mind was constantly working like clockwork, non-stop, trying to understand the fundamental problem of black people that made them so reluctant to change.

My African childhood, family, and community nurtured my worldview and the perception with which I seek to understand the world. Throughout my entire teenage years, I was groomed into looking at the world from the "Black Lens". For those of us from sub-Saharan Africa, North America, and the Caribbean, who had experienced racism in the Western world, our worldview has consequently been sharpened into more of a defensive and confrontational edge in which we surrender our willpower to the European and blame everything on the so-called "white man" and its "white supremacy". We were groomed into the idea of belief that the European white male, with long mustache and dressed like the royal guards of England, is somehow responsible for the problems of all black people. But what of the idea that we can't unite and treat each other with respect – is it because this "white man" doesn't allow it? Or has he prevented us from doing so? Anytime we think the problem is "out there", that thought is the problem. We empower what's out there to control us.[1]

Yet blacks have never challenged this notion! Black people are so spiritual that they are willing to pray to God to solve their problems, but won't put in the efforts to understand what their problems really are.

As true as this may be, the power of our mind was never taken away, though many black scholars across North America may argue to differ. The ability to make choices since post-Slavery was never stolen or deprived by anyone, nor the willpower to implement what is best for blacks.

The absurd teachings preached within the black-conscious community made me doubt my willpower, and question if the "white man" dictates my freedom of choice. To a certain degree, a lot of the black behaviors and personalities had become  racial baggage which we choose to blame on the "white man". I couldn't wait to meet this so called "white man" who was responsible for all black problems and reclaim my freedom of choice!

I began questioning:

- Why did Malcolm X and other black leaders call the white men the "devil"?
- What makes white people think they have a superior culture to blacks?
- Why are European governments so organized and Africa's not?
- Why is it that white people don't have a sense of rhythm like blacks?
- How is it that black people can be so happy and be so poor?
- Why are black people so great in music?
- Why do blacks easily influence other cultures?
- Why are blacks more religious than other races?
- Why is it that black people value material things?
- Why is it that black people embrace a flamboyant lifestyle?
- Why is it that black people are so sensitive?
- Why is it that blacks tend to have a more relaxed attitude towards time? (African time)

Asking myself these questions and continually wondering why blacks behave in these certain ways, however, put me in a state of distress to the point of falling into severe depression. I was always sad, felt hopeless, and lost motivation and interest in the things I had previously enjoyed. It even reached the point where I found it almost impossible to get through daily life.

I read the story of Viktor Frankl, a Jewish psychiatrist who was imprisoned in the death camps of Nazi Germany, where he experienced things that were so repugnant to our sense of decency that we shudder to even repeat them.

His parents, his brother, and his wife, all died in the camps or were sent to the gas chambers. Except for his sister, his entire family perished. Frankl himself suffered torture and innumerable indignities, never knowing from one moment to the next if his path would lead to the gas chamber or if he would be among the "saved" who would remove the bodies or shovel out the ashes of victims.

One day, naked and alone in a small room, he started to become aware of what he later called "the last of the human freedoms" – the freedom his Nazi captors could not take away. They could control his entire environment, they could do what they wanted to his body, but Viktor Frankl himself was a self-aware being who could look as an observer at his very involvement. His basic identity was intact. He could decide within himself how all of this was going to affect him. Between what happened to him, or the stimulus and his response to it, was his freedom or power to choose that response.

In the midst of the most degrading circumstances imaginable, Frankl used the human endowment of self-awareness to discover a fundamental principle about the nature of man: between stimulus and response, man has the freedom to choose.[2]

For about 12 months, I battled low self-esteem, with recurrent episodes of depression, but Viktor's story inspired me. Every morning, I started a "talking therapy" with myself. After washing my face with tepid water, I'd look into the mirror and stare into my soul, then tell myself out loud:

"I AM NOT DEPRESSED!"
"I AM NOT DEPRESSED!"
"I AM NOT DEPRESSED!"

Three times each day and the next day, I would repeat the same thing again:

"I AM NOT DEPRESSED!"
"I AM NOT DEPRESSED!"
"I AM NOT DEPRESSED!"

Also the day after, and so on for weeks…

Slowly but surely, by repeating the same thought over and over again, I started to feel better about myself and I began to regain my self-esteem and my confidence. Through this ability to act based on self-awareness, simply by telling myself over and over again that I wasn't depressed, I noticed that it gave me power and control over my life. My eyes opened up, I began seeing things I had never seen before, and reality unfolded itself like a blooming flower.

I applied the same technique towards racism and white supremacy, not by fighting it or accepting it, but to deny its very existence. This method shattered my whole worldview. And everything I thought I knew or had learned, were pretty useless at this stage, as they couldn't withstand the power of perception.

Sometimes we simply assume that the way we see things is the way they really are or the way they should be.[3] I adopted an open-minded attitude towards life, and particularly in issues surrounding race and black struggle. I remember the things which I used to get irritated and offended about, like the word "nigger" no longer applied to me nor were they able to trigger me to react.

In discovering the basic principles of self-awareness, I realized that we all have conscience – a deep inner awareness of right and wrong, of the principles that govern our behavior, and a sense of the degree to which our thoughts and actions are in harmony with them. We have independent will – the ability to act based on our self-awareness, free of all other influences. This is due to our unique human characteristics.

But we can write a new program for ourselves, totally separate from our instincts. This is why an animal's capacity is relatively limited and man's is unlimited. But if we live based on our conditioning and conditions, or out of our collective memory, we will become limited.[4]

A true change starts with the man in the mirror; philosophers for thousand of years had issued good advice: *KNOW THYSELF!* It's good to know our own abilities and inabilities, for this shows us areas in which we can improve. But if we only know our negative characteristics, we're in a mess, as our value becomes small.[5]

The way we see things is the source of the way we think and the way we act.[6] In regards to racial issues, black people have worked themselves into a "state of paranoia", to the point that it has become more difficult to discuss race-related topics than to fight them.

This frenzied behavior has prevented them from seeing their problem from a different perspective, and made them reluctant to accept any constructive criticism or to be open for healthy debate. Some remain stuck on the old paradigm of racial worldview, unable to exit from the blame-game of accusing the so-called "white man". They simply assume that the way they see things is the way they really are, or the way they should be, and consequently their attitudes and behaviors grow out of those assumptions.[7] As the German physicist Max Planck said: "When you change the way you look at things, the things you look at change."

What do you see in the picture here: a young woman or an old lady?

Our assumption influences our worldview, if we believe in them.

The more aware we are of our basic paradigms or assumptions, and the extent to which we have been influenced by our experience, the more we can take responsibility for those assumptions, examine them, test them against reality, then listen to others and be open to their perceptions, thereby getting a larger picture and a far more objective view. [8]

Black people need to adopt a new level of thinking. As Albert Einstein observed, "The significant problems we face cannot be solved at the same level of thinking we were at when we created them." As we look around us and within us, and recognize the problems created as we live and interact within the personality ethic, we can begin to realize that these are deep, fundamental problems that cannot be solved on the superficial level on which they were created. We need a new level, a deeper level of thinking, a paradigm based on the principles that accurately describe the territory of effective human being and interacting, to solve these deep problems. [9]

A man who prefers to be fed, will only eat the crumbs left over. As black people, we shouldn't waste time and effort on fighting racism with racism, but should reverse all our efforts and strength inwards towards self-empowerment and respect, and by starting to take responsibility for our own communities and development. Building for-self will be a more effective blow than fighting racism on the battleground for equality. Thus, no man can give another man equality unless he has possessed the same criteria in which equality can be measured. To carry on such a struggle means to be armed with unflinching courage and to be prepared for endless sacrifices. You seize the bull by the horns, you suffer many heavy blows, you are sometimes thrown to the ground, sometimes you get up with broken limbs, and only after the hardest contest does victory reward the bold. [10]

### Success Is The Best Revenge.

On numerous occasions, I tried to challenge the problem facing black people around the globe. Talking with my friends and family regarding these issues, I observed the adaptability with which they adopted different positions on the same question.[11]I don't know what horrified me the most: their perception, or their moral and ethical coarseness, or the low level of their intellectual development.[12] It was hard for me to understand people who possessed some sensible opinions when spoken to alone, but who suddenly lost them as soon as they came under the influence of the others. It's like their opinions seemed to swing back again and again to the old madness.

It was possible to cure them temporarily of this vice, but only for days or at most weeks. If later you met the man you thought you had converted, he was just the same as before! His old unnatural state had regained full possession of him.[13] To use a computer metaphor as an example, a lot of black people are programmed, and can be trained to be responsible, but they can't take responsibility for that training; in other words, they can't direct it. They can't change the programming. They are not even aware of it.[14] This may be sad to state, but to change a thing means to recognize it first. [15]

As human beings, we are responsible for our own lives. Our behavior is a function of our decisions, not our conditions. We have the initiative and responsibility to make things happen. By nature, we are proactive, but if our lives are a function of the conditioning and conditions, it is because we have, by conscious decision or by default, chosen to empower those things to control us. In making such a choice, we become reactive. Reactive people are often affected by their physical and social environment; when people treat them well, they feel well. If the weather is good, they feel good. In addition, reactive people build their emotional lives around the behavior of others, empowering the weaknesses of other people to control them.

The word responsibility – "response-ability" – is the ability to choose your response. Highly proactive people recognize that responsibility. They do not blame circumstances, conditions, or conditioning for their behavior. Their behavior is a product of their own conscious choice, rather than a product of their conditions. Proactive people can carry their own weather with them; whether it rains or shines makes no difference to them.

As Gandhi observed, "They cannot take away our self respect if we do not give it to them." Or in the words of Eleanor Roosevelt, "No one can hurt you without your consent." It is our willing permission, our consent to what happens to us, that hurts us far more than what happens to us in the first place. [16]

It became clear to me that the deepest sense of our social responsibility for the creation of better foundations for our development, must be combined with brutal determination in breaking down these incurable tumors. That is preventing us from starting a healthier channel for future development.[17]

One day, whilst I was sitting on a chair in the kitchen, I began thinking about what resonates with being black and what doesn't. I sat there for hours and hours thinking about what could explain the "black problem" and what could be changed in order to find the solution to resolve the problem that we were facing as a race. And all of a sudden... BINGO!

I stated that in order for me to understand the "black problem", I must look at the condition from a different perspective, one which I was not used to seeing. I wanted to study and observe what the "black problem" would look like from the prospective of the so-called "white man"(as far as I know they are the ones with whom we compete and compare ourselves). So I adopted my "white lens" to peak at the black struggle through a white perspective by applying abstract thinking.

I began analyzing everything that made me black. Sometimes I would observe my mother and examine certain things she did, and then correlate these traits and behaviors with blacks across North America and the Caribbean. I observed and analyzed every single thing that black people do, from the way they talk, walk, and conduct themselves, the music they make and listen to, the way they dance, the way they dominate in physical activities, the way they influence other cultures, and how successful they are in the entertainment business.

What I began discovering after many months of analyzing these traits and patterns, was a mind-blowing and paradigm shift. I discovered that black people possessed a huge amount of:

*EMOTIONAL RESERVOIR.*

This Emotional Reservoir can be traced back to African history since the beginning of human evolution.

This has been their CORE INTELLIGENCE that has guided their intuition and helped them to thrive better in areas of music, sport, rhythm, entertainment, life, and social skills.

This same Emotional Reservoir, I discovered, was also the source of certain patterns of behaviors that were found among the black racial group. Blacks tend to have very strong personalities and are more extrovert than other races.

I also observed the differences between blacks' and whites' behaviors, and I noticed that white people tend to have a lower Emotional Reservoir than blacks. This lower Emotional Reservoir is responsible for why whites live stressful lives, suffer more depression and anxiety, and have higher suicide rates than blacks.

The lack of this Emotional Reservoir is the reason why white people tend to lack the ability to fully grasp and understand senses of rhythm and emotion. They dance as though somebody had trained them – left, one, two; right, three, four; the same steps and patterns over and over. But with black people, nobody in the world could have choreographed the way they dance; they do whatever they feel from the music.[18]

If one observes whites, one can clearly see that they depend more on their intellect. The intellect has become the CORE of White Intelligence; whites heavily rely on their intellect to understand and solve life problems, including music, and they barely understand it or know how to express such emotions. Whites tend to have an emotionless (lacking feelings) culture and behavior, and are known to be cold. I have heard other non-white racial groups say that the white race has little emotion, lacks social skills, and have a closed-up culture.

I continue to observe the differences between blacks and whites, and other ethnic groups. I found that the East Asians tend to have even a lower Emotional Reservoir than whites.

All ethnic groups depend on the intellect and emotions, but what I found that there are some ethnic groups that depend on the emotion more than the intellect, while others depend on the intellect more than emotion. In this respect, whites and East Asians (Chinese, Japanese, and Koreans, etc.) depend on their intellect more than emotions. East Asians tend to be very introvert and show far lower emotions than whites, particularly in the areas such as music and social skills, and they have a very closed culture.

Blacks, on the other hand, tend to have an open culture.

Having a higher Emotional Reservoir, blacks are able to easily influence whites and other non-white groups more than they influence blacks. As people who have higher Emotional Reservoir can influence many others, that's why black culture had become the most dominant and popular culture in the world.

A person can be intellectual, but another person can be less intellectual and can express his emotions strongly. The person who has the stronger emotional center will usually be able to connect with more people emotionally and mentally. If you can influence a person emotionally, then on average you will be able to influence them mentally. The ability to appeal to a person's intellect first does not guarantee you will be able to influence them emotionally. When emotions are active, then a person will behave according to the emotions inside them.

As much as white and East Asian cultures are admired for their intellectual and technological achievements, black culture still dominates and touches the emotional centers of all ethnic groups across the globe in a way that other cultures do not. This includes music, sports, entertainment, clothing, verbal expression, body language, hairstyles, "swagger", and fashion. Activities where emotions are highly required is when blacks are given opportunities, like in music, dancing, boxing, sport, and other areas where the whites have fallen short in emotional performances.

The African-American culture is more popular than any other culture in America, mainly because black people connect and appeal to the emotions of other racial groups. White culture, on the other hand, only appeals to the intellect of other racial groups but not heavily to their emotions. In general, African-American culture, with its powerful emotional influence, is the culture that helps unite America. No other ethnic group's culture unites Americans of all racial groups like the African-American culture. The cultures of other ethnic groups currently living in America cannot unite all Americans either — only the black culture has been able to do this.

During times of racial segregation and oppression in North America, blacks were still able to influence and penetrate the white culture, despite the barriers of racism and discrimination, simply because blacks appeal to the emotional sense of Western culture which it couldn't have been possible to influence through logic or with the power of reasoning. That's because the intellect is known to be cold and emotionless, but the emotional center has feelings – and feelings make you feel alive. Feelings, whether positive or negative, will cause you to act and behave according to the feelings in you at a given moment. Blacks depend on the intellect, too, but they are more influenced by their emotions.

I found that black people in general depend on emotional connections more than intellect connections. This explains why, when blacks come together and deal with each other on a political level or social level (community) to accomplish a particular agenda, if there is no strong emotional connection they will not put forth the necessary effort to accomplish the task. Another example is that when there are two black politicians running for office, the one that can appeal to the emotions of the black voters usually wins, even if he or she has no solid ideas that can potentially help the black voters.

The lack of discovering this Intelligence is what has caused blacks to be under-developed and to under-achieve compared to the Western world. I beg to differ from the assumption that the reason why black nations couldn't thrive as well as Europe was due to lower IQ or racism.

My thesis suggests that the lack of understanding of their CORE Intelligence (Emotional Reservoir) has been the main drawback of these black nations. Although blacks study as hard as the Europeans or East Asians, the overall impact of their Core of Intelligence will influence how the knowledge is received in the brain. In this scenario, blacks tend to find it harder than whites or East Asians to implement what they have learned. This is not because they are deficient; it's simply because they are different.

Blacks have a different Core of Intelligence that is their emotional ability to understand and to fully grasp and interpret whatever they have learned into their emotional senses. In other words, if doesn't make sense to their emotions, it does not make sense at all.

I also discovered that a lot of behavioral problems that were affecting many black communities, churches, and nations, were the result of blacks having a higher Emotional Reservoir Unbalanced. The power of this Emotional Reservoir can either produce negative or positive, toxic or non-toxic emotional outbursts that are highly contagious and unpredictable. The unbalanced effect of this Emotional Reservoir leads to some "bad" personalities and traits that are found among blacks; this makes them act and behave the way they do in a way that others might consider irrational or pathological. Blacks in sub-Saharan Africa, North America, Europe, and in the Caribbean, are victims of this undiscovered Emotional Reservoir.

The unbalanced effect of this Emotional Reservoir is the reason why a lot of blacks are:

- Easily irritated
- Overly impulsive
- Overly sensitive
- Over spending
- Too fearful
- Having family problems

And many also tend to get into trouble easily with employers, crime, violence, anger, envy, jealousy, hatred-related tendencies, and lack caution in many situations. I discovered that a lot of these behaviors found within the black communities were because they were simply driven, controlled, and influenced by their emotions.

For example, in *Do or Die*, journalist Leon Bing reports on reasons given by gang members for killing people:

"Cause I don't like his attitude."

"Cause of the way he walk."

"Cause he try to get with my lady."

"Cause he give me no respect."

"Cause he is a disgrace."

"Cause he wearing the wrong color."

"Cause I don't like him."

"Cause he said somethin' wrong."

"Cause he look at me funny." [19]

Black people are not even aware of or understand the power of this Emotional Reservoir. Too often many blacks tend to struggle with controlling themselves or to act appropriately, and this emotionally-driven behavior has caused many wars amongst tribes and religious groups, creating instabilities in sub-Saharan Africa.

The unbalanced effect of this emotion makes them act out of character, speak too loud, and act extremely violently or aggressively, but by doing so they allow themselves to be ridiculed, controlled, and manipulated by those who find these behaviors a sign of weakness. So, they find themselves manipulated and used against themselves by those who want to oppress and control them to benefit from their culture and their emotional abilities. Pitching the old vs. the young, Igbo vs. Yoruba, dark-skinned vs. light-skinned...

For example, HIP HOP started as a voice to fight against oppression and injustice, but decades later the culture was subverted and used against blacks by promoting gang-related activities, drugs use, and crime. As a result of this 'Ideological Subversion', many blacks find themselves being involved in gangs, drugs, and criminal activities, which in the long run has served those that benefit from black oppression and the prison industrial complex. This has occurred to the extent that blacks do not have a say in the music or things that they have invented, nor do they own it, distribute it, or control it.

They have simply used the power of logic (applied psychology) to manipulate the black emotions (weaknesses) in this regard, to control black people and keep them under their thumb. They tend to hire blacks, deliberately manipulate their emotions, and use it to make profit while blacks still remain poor and bamboozled. But even blacks are unaware of the Emotional Power that they possess. They remain aloof and bamboozled while their culture, emotion, and music has been subverted and used against them with the help of their own free will.

# HUNTERS IN A SOCIETY
# OF FARMERS

The African sense of community is conditioned by the cultural and social institutions of centuries which empower an individual's worth, while the European has a little awareness of this concept. For example, anyone who has ever witnessed a ceremonial African dance will certainly agree that the individual's sense of personal power and worth is immeasurably heightened by the communal nature of the event.[1]

Ancient civilization saw man always as part of society, and society as embedded in nature and dependent upon cosmic forces. For them, nature and man did not stand in opposition and did not, therefore, have to be apprehended by different mode cognition... natural phenomenon were regularly conceived in terms of human experience, and that human experience was conceived in terms of cosmic events.[2]

In African religion, and in many other primary religion formulations, it is the spiritual-emotional needs of the people within the culture that are served. At the same time, the values of the culture are sanctioned, and the mechanisms for its continuance are sacralized. Spiritual/philosophical conceptions such as ancestor communion, which help to explain the universe as a spiritual whole in which all life and being are periodically regenerated, give the Africans an emotional security and confidence that the Europeans lack. But such conceptions did not prepare the African, nor the Native American or Oceanic counterparts, to deal politically with the invasion of the Europeans.

The ancient cultures sought to use the forces of the universe to ensure a harmonious existence.[3] The Europeans did not understand the African spirituality and they interpreted the true place of human origin as a universal state of ignorance, full of darkness, and their blackness to be threatening and evil. The blackness indeed was the spiritual, metaphysical realm to which Europeans had little if any access. The "dark side" of things was the inner vision of the unconscious that opened the door to communication with ancestral symbols and wisdom.[4]

Ancient cultures and civilization in Africa, America, and Australia, depended on emotion more than intellect. Even isolated tribes who live in various parts of the world understand the importance of emotional connections with the universe. For example, when a Shoshone (Native American) looked about for food, he listened to what the land told him, the voices of the plants and animals, and the Earth itself. They showed and told him where his day's meal would be found, and also what types of ceremony would be appropriate to thank the world for this gift. [5]

The initial encounter between Europeans and "non-European" people inevitably emphasized these differences, as they describe: anything they have, if it be asked for, they never say no but rather invite the person to accept it, and show so much lovingness as though they would give their heart.

Africans and other cultures invariably seek to include the Europeans in their system of gift-exchange, offering him love and peace.[6] Their culture does not teach them to mistrust others.

As Europeans came face-to-face with Africans, they narrated the remarkable experience they found. Blacks are not racist towards other races. Blacks are not afraid of ethnic contacts. Whites are.[7] When non-whites encounter white culture, they intuitively sense and know (the behavior of some whites also assist in this) that whites do not accept them as equal. Anyone can be a part of white culture but whites as a collective don't accept him or her as equal. This is because whites view their culture as more advanced than the average non-white culture. This feeling of not being viewed as an equal creates a feeling of rejection with the average non-white person; it makes them feel like a second-class citizen and an outsider. But black general culture and black sub-culture makes you feel welcomed, and it creates a strong emotional connection with people. Black culture does not make the average person from another ethnicity feel like an outsider. In fact, as it turns out, one of the weaknesses of black civilization during the medieval times, was their openness, the cosmopolitanism of these societies. The medieval black kingdoms were open to people of all horizons. And today, one of the basic weaknesses of African societies is that they still maintain this inherited cosmopolitan trait.[8]

European philosophers before Plato and the Western Renaissance, believed that there was a world of "One" which connected man with God and was known as "Consciousness"; something all ancient civilization from Africa, and others around the world, had talked about for thousands of years.

Professor Julian Jaynes puts forth the concept that in prehistoric times (more than 7,000 to 10,000 years ago) people actually heard the voices of the Gods. When they looked out into the natural world, they saw fairies, sprites, spirits, and other entities. Professor Jaynes in *The Origin of Consciousness in the Breakdown of the Bicameral Mind* posits that the two hemispheres of the brain were more fully connected, that the auditory regions of the left hemisphere were directly connected to the right hemisphere.[9]

For most of our history, mankind in some way believed in the existence of the other, invisible world, inaccessible to the senses. It is only in relatively recent times that this knowledge has been rejected as unreal and placed all our faith in the truths of modern science. Yet not everyone has been happy with this conclusion; traces of this other knowledge remain, and many persist in trying to understand it and what it can tell us about ourselves.

The proponents of modern science insist this is a mistake and assure us that we must reject this false knowledge in order to gain the truth. For those who have a sense of this invisible, other reality, the answers to life's mysteries offered by modern science are inadequate and unsatisfying. They are unable to accept them, and they find themselves seeking something else. For our scientific kind of knowledge, the spirit or souls are superstitions or delusions, as neither can be detected by the senses. Who has seen the soul or the spirit?

The African tradition says that there is another kind of knowledge. It is not one of physical facts, nor can it be quantified and measured.

In the African ancient tradition, the physical world available to the senses that science affirms as the only reality is only a small part of a much greater reality – an invisible, inner reality that informs the outer world and gives it life. It is a knowledge of our inner world, not the outer one. A knowledge of what we used to call the spirit or the soul. That invisible, intangible something that animates us and leads us to ask questions about who we are and what our place in this mysterious world can be. It is essentially concerned with the meaning of our existence, a question that the modern science cannot answer or rejects as nonsense. [10]

The question one must ask is, why was this knowledge rejected in the modern Western world? The central reason why this knowledge was rejected is that it fails to meet the criteria of "real" knowledge set by modern science. Since its beginning in the seventeenth century, modern science has focused on the kind of "facts" that can be grasped by the senses and proven by measurement. They abandoned the religious explanations for the world, which posited an unseen God behind the universe; accepted only that which they could see and touch; and brought an acute analysis to the phenomena of the physical world. Gradually, and with increasing certainty, they came to the conclusion that the only knowledge worth knowing was the kind that could be quantified.[11] Physical laws that could be observed and measured would, they believed, account for everything. And the belief that anything else was needed or that anything could escape the necessities imposed by these laws, was abandoned.

They formed, as the historian James Webb called it, a body of "rejected knowledge", whereby the intellectuals refused and abandoned the superstitions of the past in order to embrace the science of the modern day.[12] Professor Jaynes suggests that it was the rise of the Mesopotamian city-state empire and its use of written language that was largely responsible for the breakdown of this connection between the two hemispheres of the brain, causing all of us to lose contact with much of the right hemisphere during our normal waking consciousness.[13]

In the African view of the human, the emotional-spiritual and rational-material are inextricably bound together and, if anything, it is the human being's spirituality that defines her as human, providing the context within which she is able to create art as well as technology. Such a view leads to a very different emphasis in artistic expression. The emotional identification with, and participation in, the art form by the person and the community, are primary values that help to determine its shape. In this way the form itself becomes less of an "object". [14]

The truth is that we are all potential visionaries. In the African concepts, harmony is achieved through the balance of complementary forces, and it is indeed impossible to have a functioning whole without harmonious interaction and the existence of balancing pairs. While in the Western world, Plato recognized that in order for Europe to create and become an "ideal state", reason must control emotion.

The key is control. Clearly, according to Plato, reason is positive, valued, and higher, while emotion is negative, devalued, and more basic because it has the tendency to control us. Such control is an indication of powerlessness. It is politically unwise and undesirable; it is morally reprehensible. Better people are more reasonable and less emotional. [15]

In the State, the highest controls the lowest. The society is based on "collectives" that are "functional to specialized ends", and each individual is suited to one task or mode of participation in the State. A person will be "rewarded" for thinking in the valued mode, and such habits of thought will be reinforced in the formalized learning and socialization processes. The same person will be "punished" for thinking in the "devalued" mode, and will fail for doing so. [16] The human being who has gained control of himself and possesses the power of reason should control and dominate those whose reasoning abilities are judged to be less.

A very strong theme in the European moral and political philosophy is the idea that human beings are superior to other animals, and that they must protect that superiority in order to be truly humans. [17] Plato suggests that we are not whole beings, but rather made up of parts that are in continual conflict with one another. The person is constantly "at war" within himself, and he is not properly human until his reason controls his emotion.[18] He believes that we are made up of reason and intellect, and our better nature should control our desires, emotions, and put our senses to proper use.

The ancient African and Greek cultures viewed the world and the universe as cosmos and a "subject" to which we are all linked. Plato proposed a revolution in thought: that the universe is not "subject", but "object"; that we are not a part of it but separated from it. He said that in order to know, we must detach ourselves from what we wish to know.[19]

It was also celebrated by Aristotle in his writings on how the universe and natural world were merely collections of simple particles (atoms) that humans could manipulate once they understood them. This was refined by Descartes, who argued that the entire universe was a giant machine, and this machine-like nature echoed all the way down to the smallest level. If we could just figure out where the levers and switches were, we could always figure out a way to control the machine.[20]

It has since become a characteristic of European culture to be associated with abstract thinking (objectivity). With this knowledge came power, and then the knower – in control of his emotions by denial of its existence – can manipulate the object.[21] By eliminating or gaining control of our emotions, we can become aware of ourselves as thinking subjects, distinct from the contemplated object. Through this separation, this remoteness, this denial of cosmic relationship, we achieve "objectification" – a necessary achievement if we are to be capable of scientific cognition.

To think properly about an object, to gain knowledge of mastery over an object, we must control it. We can only do this if we are emotionally detached from it. And we gain this emotional distance from the object by first and foremost gaining control over ourselves; that is, by placing our reason (intellect) in control of our emotions (feelings). [22] In doing so, the citizens' senses were trusted less and less, until European culture ended up at one end of the spectrum, with Africa on the other. Europeans are trained neither to use their senses nor to be perceptive, where as Africans relate to the universe using sense perceptions as highly developed tools that are valued parts of the human intellectual apparatus. [23]

Researchers discovered that 3,000 years ago Africa was almost entirely populated by thousands of different (genetically and in language) tribes of hunter/gatherer people. Population density was low, strife was minimal, and the indigenous hunting people often had conflict with neighbors over borders and territories. But these conflicts served to strengthen the cultural and independent identities of both tribes involved.

Then a group of Bantu-speaking agriculturists in the northwestern part of Africa were apparently infected with a "Cultural Mental Illness" – what Professor of Native American Studies Jack Forbes calls the *Wetiko*. The Bantu-speaking farmers of northwest Africa culturally contaminated by *Wetiko* systematically spread across the entire African continent over a 2000-year period, destroying every group in their path. Professor Forbes believed that *Wetiko* (a native American term for the amoral and predatory behavior of the European invaders) originated in Mesopotamia around 5,000 years ago. From there, it spread across Fertile Crescent and into Syria, eventually infecting northern Africa, Asia, Europe, and the Americas with the arrival of Columbus. The result is that now less than one percent of the entire African continent populations are hunter/gatherers, and the languages and cultures of thousands of tribes have been lost forever.

For example, take the story of Ik – a group of hunter/gatherer people in Uganda whose rates of life-threatening psychological and physical illnesses exploded when they were forcibly moved from their natural hunting grounds and forced to engage in agriculture. Entire ethnic groups were wiped out and have now vanished from the Earth. And so, over the past 5000 years, on every continent hunters have been wiped out, displaced, slaughtered, exterminated, and oppressed by the **Wetiko** farmers/industrialists. The **Wetiko** warfare, where every last person in the "competing" tribes is put to death, is something that no anthropologist has ever found in the history or behavior of any past or modern non-**Wetiko** hunting/gathering people. The **Wetiko**, however, view non-**Wetiko** humans as exploitable and have history littered with genocide, slavery, and exploitation.[24]

Ever since Europe has become synonymous with "Modern", they syntactically made European culture into a representation of a universal stage in human development. Thereby other non-Europeans and Africans must become "Modern" before they can deal with them. Europeans are, in this view, the only ones with the authority to criticize their culture, and the criticisms they make and the solutions they find are said to have universal significance. European imperialism, in this way, is not seen as the product of the behavioral patterns of a particular cultural group nor of certain kinds of people, but rather of the natural tendencies of all people at a particular period of cultural development. Those who begin with the assumption that they are simply dealing with the character of "Modernity" are doomed from the start, for they have already accepted the terms of European ideology.[25] Basically:

*"Every culture becomes European as it becomes more Modern."*

When white European explorers left Europe, they conquered other countries and brought "these cultures" with them. They created a system based on the assumption that whites are "superior" due to their intellect (separation from nature). In the fifteenth and sixteenth centuries, Europeans not only colonized most of the world, but they also colonized information about the world. They declared most things primitive that they could not understand.[26]

For example, when the early European/American settlers fanned out across the prairies and killed every buffalo they could find. They looked at the Indians and thought they were crazy not to take and eat all the buffalo they could, and asked how could they have sat on this valuable resource for 10,000 years and not used it? They had to be savages, uncivilized half-humans who didn't have the good sense to know how to use nature's bounty for the good of the human race.[27] The Native Americans watched in shock and horror at what they considered a senseless act of insanity. How could the settlers take the life of the plains? How could they parcel up the flesh of Mother Earth? How could they be so crazy as to cut down every tree in sight? [28]

The Europeans, in their conquest of the minds of most of mankind, have been able to convince themselves and others that they are indispensable to civilization, and without them it would not have existed. Rudyard Kipling saw the "White Man's Burden" as a mandate to lift brown, black, and yellow people up to the level of white people as if whites were the norm and black, brown, and yellow people were abnormal subspecies, on a lower level.[29]

*"Why are we bent on forcing upon them a civilization not suited to them, and which only means, in their view, degradation and a loss of self-respect, which is worse than the loss of life itself?"*
Senator Tillman

Europeans have influenced the world based on what they think of themselves, and this has affected our world and everything we know to date. Therefore, the concept of race that now plagues the whole world is an artificial European invention. Professor Ashley Montagu has referred to it as "man's greatest myth". While the word race and the concepts around it are artificial, the effects of its creation are real. The application of this concept has affected the lives of people in most parts of the world. It was part of the basis of the slave trade and the colonial system. [30]

For Plato and those whom he influenced, the intellect (left-brain) is an indispensable tool for surviving in the world, and is the reason why they have become the dominant species on the planet. The white cultures have a long list of intellectuals that have shaped European cultures for many centuries. These intellectuals contributed to European politics and philosophy. Some qualities of European thought are unique; certain ideas occurred only to Europeans, and certain techniques were discovered and applied only by them. European culture embraces their unity, based on what they have in common rather than their differences. [31] The descendants of Europeans who live in countries like the United States of America, Canada, Australia, and New Zealand, have continued this culture and behaviors that have helped them to build modern societies. Today, white societies are dominated in all areas by intellect; seldom do they depend or allow emotions/ feelings to dictate things in their societies.

According to Dr. Iain McGilchrist, one result of this left-brain (intellect) behavior takeover is that the materialist, reductionist science increasingly diminishes the right-brain (emotion) contribution to our understanding of the world. One example of this is the mainstream neuroscience's contention that the right brain is minor, secondary, and ultimately unimportant. The right brain is geared toward engaging with living things, and with recognizing overall patterns, meanings, and relations. It is attuned to the network of connections that links everything with everything else. Its fundamental attention is to the "Whole". It is more geared to perceiving the forest, we might say, and not the individual trees.

The left-brain, on the other hand – literally – is geared towards breaking up the whole that the right brain presents. It turns the right brain's unity into bits and pieces, which it can then manipulate. Its job is to analyze the big picture presented by the right and reduce it to easily manageable parts, which it can control and arrange to suit its purposes. These are generally geared toward survival.

Where the right-brain is open to "newness" and appreciates the "being" of things in themselves, the left-brain is geared to representing reality as something familiar and sees things in terms of their use. The left-brain has a utilitarian approach to reality, whereas the right brain just accepts things as they are. The left-brain "stands apart" from experience; it distances itself from it in order to focus with dazzling clarity on discreet bits, and loses the connections between things. The left-brain ever since has been busy creating a mechanical environment, a world of parts, bits, and pieces, that it can manipulate, and through which it can fulfill its utilitarian aims and goals at the expense of the whole.[32]

All of this points to an increasingly left-brain world, creating modern cities, vast industrialized areas, the seemingly unstoppable digitizing of experience. Think of the growing demand for the "lifelike" presentation of entertainment, of HD television and 3-D films, that represent to us in electronically enhanced detail a "natural world" that is itself steadily diminishing.[33] Ever since, they have created a society that is disempowering for their own gain. A society where death –dealing substances like tobacco, drugs, and alcohol – became a part of daily existence. Where murderers, Mafia, and corrupted leaders can live in expensive houses in "nice" neighborhoods and get praise for it. A society that takes from the poor to give to the rich and wealthy; where students are trapped in insane bank loans, and home loans carry an increasing interest rate to profit the rich. A "dog eat dog" culture where government officials are corrupted by power, greed, and are ego-driven, and where it has become the norm that in order to be successful in business one must lie and cheat.

For example, in the business world, it is well known that if you can convince people something is wrong with them, you can then make a lot money selling them a remedy. It's been done with facial and leg hair, wrinkles, and other ordinary human conditions. Convince people there's something wrong with or embarrassing about their normal functions, and get rich by selling them mouthwash, bleaching creams, fake hair, wrinkle removers, diet pills, and a host of other products. The exploiters on the fringes of the medical arena depend on the notion of sickness or abnormality to peddle their wares. To sell, they depend on convincing you that there's something about you that's intolerable, something that is wrong, something you need to change. Their message is not, "If you feel you have a problem, I have some solutions that may work." Rather, it is, "You are sick and I am not, and you must unquestioningly let me help you with my cure." If we question the treatment, our intentions are challenged: "Why are you questioning me when I'm only trying to help you?" [34]

In today's society the entire Western educational system is created in the conformity of the European (left-brain) objective learning style. Since the release of *The Bell Curve* by Herrnstein & Murray, many Western psychologists believe that the reason Africans and others, like the isolated tribes of other parts of the world, were not as successful as Europeans was due to their lower IQ scores. This idea continues to persist in the Western fields of psychology, with the assumption that the larger the brain's size, the more neurons and synapses the brain has, which means that whites and Eastern Asians are more intelligent than blacks.

The IQ debate became worldwide, even though IQ tests were mainly developed for use in the American/European culture. Many Europeans and Americans believe that the higher IQ they have, the better chance they have to be successful. In many Western schools, many black children are labeled as deficient due to their ways of learning and the differences in their behaviors. In doing so, many schools came up with meaningless solutions like Ritalin, and labeled these pupils as being EMH (Educable Mentally Handicapped), TMH (Trainable Mentally Handicapped), or having ADD (Attention Deficit Disorder). They could not understand why black children were having problems learning from an "object" in the same way as the European children, so they assumed they were deficient. They are taught to see others who are different as being deficient. Whites saw blacks who are predominantly right-brained as being deficient.

The Reverend Jeremiah Wright in 2008 stated: "White people are left-brained while Africans and African-Americans are right-brained, subject-oriented in their learning style, they have a different way of learning and have a different tonality."

76

In Dr. Janice Hale's book, *Black Children: Their Roots, Culture and Learning Style,* she showed us that in comparing African-American children and European-American children in the field of education, we were comparing apples and rocks. Dr. Hale's research led her to stop comparing African-American children with European-American children, and she started comparing the pedagogical methodologies of African-American children to African children and European-American children to European children. And she discovered that the two different worlds have two different ways of learning. However, different is not synonymous with deficient.

European and European-American children have a left-brained, cognitive, object-oriented learning style. Left-brain is logical, and analytical, object-oriented means the student learns from an object.

African and African-American children have a different way of learning. They are right-brained, subject-oriented in their learning style. Right-brain means creative and intuitive. Subject-oriented means they learn from a subject, not an object. They learn from a person and from what they see.

In other words, Africans have a higher visual learning ability. They learn from a subject, not from an object, because they came from a culture of story-telling, imagery, and symbols. They have a different way of learning because they come from a right-brained creative oral culture, like the (Griots) in Africa who can go for two or three days as oral repositories of a people's history, and like the oral tradition which passed down the first five books in the Jewish, Christian, and the Hebrew bible, long before there was a written Hebrew script or alphabet.[35] Older cultures are older because they have survived for tens of thousands of years. In comparison, modern cultures are still an experiment.[36]

The **Wetiko** domination continues in our modern world; today Europeans have shifted the entire world on the path to hell. They made an Earth-wide attempt to destroy ancient knowledge and people, intentionally domesticated, taken out of nature and brutalized, to be poor copies of Europeans. Most people think that the white race is progressing, improving, growing and evolving with new knowledge, new inventions, new technologies, and new discoveries. Now blacks and brown people of the world are blindly following their footsteps as though the European worldview and reality is absolute and the right way to live on the planet. As in the past (eg, Sumer, Rome, Greece), however great its grandeur, it has self-destructed, while older tribes have survived for thousands of years.[37]

Sigmund Freud is the father of psychoanalysis, and the man to whom many today look for definition of what is "sick" and what is "healthy" mentally. He pointed out that what modern civilization refers to as a "healthy ego" is, in fact, "a shrunken residue". This shrinking into separateness, this breaking of the intimate bond with the natural world around us, has separated us into isolated "boxes". This explains why many white societies have more mental-related illness compared to non-white societies. Many psychologists presume that one result of this "shrinking process" is that the third most common cause of death for Americans between 15 and 27 years of age, according to the National Institutes of Mental Health, is suicide. [38]

If we are to survive, we must relearn the true history of the world as our ancestors understood it, and we must plot a course of the hell that they have forced unto all of us. We must return to living in balance with creation, just as our ancestors lived. Many of us only know what we're exposed to. We refuse to question the illusion that surrounds us; we refuse to question what they tell us. We develop emotional attachments to things that give us a false sense of hope and make us "feel" better temporarily.

Most of our people are still asleep because of high intensity and silent low intensity warfare being waged on us. Some of us may take longer to get shaken into awaken consciousness, and some may stay asleep forever. This keeps us trapped in the illusion and the hell they have created on earth.

So, in order to live in a truly balanced and sustainable world, we must start creating a community by withdrawing our life energy from this illusion. Everything our people are doing now, like fighting racism and white supremacy, is only a reactionary measure. This means that everything that we are doing is only in reaction to what is being done to us, and not what we did originally. We know what system needs to be created to enable us to live in a peaceful, abundant, and balanced society like the one older cultures had for hundreds of thousands of years before it was destroyed by the modern science.

We can see the results of this around us everywhere, from the computer I am using to write this book to the probes we have sent into space in order to explore the mysteries of the universe.[39]

To say that this kind of knowledge is good and useful is an understatement. Our problems derive not from our technology, our diet, violence in the media, or any other thing we do. They arise out of our culture – our view of the world.

The reason most solutions offered to the world's crisis are impractical is because they arise from the same worldview that caused the problem. Recycling won't save the world; birth control won't save the world; and saving what little is left of the rainforests won't save the world. Even if all those good things were fully implemented, our fundamental problem would still remain, and will inevitably be repeated. Even cold fusion and the elimination of the need for oil will not save the world.

Nothing but changing our way of seeing and understanding the world can produce real, meaningful, and lasting change... and that change in perspective will naturally lead us to begin to control our populations, save our forests, re-create community, and reduce our wasteful consumption.[40] When enough people change the way they view things, solutions become evident, often in ways we couldn't even imagine. We have destroyed much of the world because of our culture; we can save much of it by changing our culture.[41]

In this context, being the "Hunters in a Society of Farmers", Africans are faced with difficulties, and the effect is already seen in the prison systems, the schools, and on the streets. But it is totally disempowering to say: everything is okay with the Modern society; it must be the Africans that are seriously screwed-up, less intelligent, and need treatment. That subjugates them, and robs them off their dignity and humanity. It is *Wetiko!*

# EMOTIONAL RESERVOIR

The Emotional Reservoir is a reservoir of energy that people absorb from the sun. The sun is by far the most important source of energy for life on Earth. This energy is ultimately transferred to all living organisms. Plants directly convert sunlight into chemical energy via photosynthesis. Humans convert sunlight into energy to suit their purposes. When you spend too much time in the sun, you will feel how much energy your body absorbed.

The point of all this is the fact that the sun is a natural power source, which helps to improve health and make one feel happier. The sun has a powerful influence on the physical and mental lives of human beings. The sun emits visible energy like light, heat, ultraviolet rays, and x-rays. Ultraviolet light affects the human body in a number of ways. One of the greatest health benefits is the production of vitamin D, which is essential to calcium metabolism and the formation of bone.

The ultraviolet light has several therapeutic effects and a positive psychological effect. Human civilization required energy to function; the sun has profoundly influenced human intellect and custom. For many people, the sun formed the basis of their culture, agriculture, religion, and ceremonial lives.

Sunlight gives you more energy, boosts fertility, reduces the risk of cancer, encourages the production of white cells, which helps to boost the immune system and fight infection. And higher levels of serotonin in the body not only makes you feel happier, but it also suppresses the appetite, so that's why you eat less in warmer weather.

The sun has been the energy generator for the planet since the beginning of time, and is responsible for our complexion, mood, and many other things on earth. This means the closer contact one has with sunlight, then the more energy one absorbs from it, and reserves within oneself. And those who are less close to the sunlight absorb and reserve less energy.

The darker the skin complexion, the more emotional reservoir there is and the higher the sensitivity of this energy compared to the lighter pigmentation. The darker the skin complexion, the closer they are or were to the sunlight.

In dark-skinned individuals, melanin is distributed throughout all the skin's layers and is stored for longer periods of time. Melanin is responsible for giving skin color due to the energy absorbed. The melanin is very sensitive, that is why under distress or inflammation there is an increase in the production and transfer of melanin. This is also known within the scientific field as a mood-enhancer, as the closer humans are to the sunlight, which is an energy generator, the happier and better life they tend to live. Psychologists believe the decrease in sunlight exposure is associated with Seasonal Affective Disorder (SAD) and depression. This explains why black societies have a lower rate of depression than non-black societies.

The Emotional Reservoir, which is then transformed into melanin, carries these three characteristics of Melanin Effects:

1.  **Higher Emotion**

    Blacks carry energetic radiation more than any other races on the planet. Due to the fact that they evolved in Africa, they had more contact with the sun, and the energy that they radiate has also been the invisible driving force which has helped them to thrive throughout history. This has given blacks an extra edge in the area where emotions are highly influenced, like culture, dancing, music, and art performances. Blacks have proven to be more sociable, more outgoing, more impulsive, more dominant, better in music/rhythmic melody and dancing than other races.

    Professor of Psychology, J. Philippe Ruston suggests that blacks are more socially active and more outgoing than whites and Orientals. Daniel Goleman in his book, *Emotional Intelligence,* also wrote about this trait which he experienced with an African-American bus driver. He said, "The memory of that encounter has stayed with me for close to twenty years. When I rode that Madison Avenue bus, the driver, a middle-aged black man with an enthusiastic smile, who welcomed me with a friendly, 'Hi, how you doing?' startled me. A greeting he proffered to everyone else who entered the bus. And yet, imagining the spreading virus of good feeling that must have rippled through city, starting from passengers on his bus, I saw that this bus driver was an urban peacemaker of sorts, wizard-like in his power to transmute the sullen irritability that seethed in his passengers, to soften and open their hearts. Psychological science knew little or nothing of the mechanics of emotion."[1]

## 2. Strength & Physical Features

Blacks who evolved in tropical Africa tend to have stronger bones and more physical strength compared to whites and Asians who evolved in colder environments. The sun keeps the bones healthy because the body produces vitamin D when exposed to the sunlight. The so-called "sunlight vitamin" helps the body to absorb calcium, which is essential for stronger bones. These physical differences can be seen in sport, athletics, and other physical exercise where strength is required.

According to Jon Entine's book, *Taboo: Why Black Athletes Dominate Sports and Why We Are Afraid to Talk About It,* white men can't jump. Asian men can't either. Black men – and women – sure can.[2] Compared to whites, blacks have narrower hips, which gives them a more efficient stride. They have wider shoulders, less body fat, and more muscle. Their muscles include more fast-twitch muscles, which produce power. They have a shorter sitting height, which provides a higher center of gravity and better balance.

His book also shows that these physical advantages give blacks the edge in sports like boxing, basketball, football, and sprinting. Entine points out that in sports, blacks have a genetic edge.

J. Philippe Rushton, Professor of Psychology, posits that blacks have from 3 to 19% more testosterone than whites and Orientals. The testosterone translates into more explosive energy. The testosterone gives blacks an edge at sports, making them restless.[3]

### 3. Genetic

Blacks genetically carry more of this energy dominance than whites and Orientals who have absorbed less of the sunlight energy due to their environment. In interracial babies, the melanin effect appears more genetically dominant in the characteristics of the child. For example, Barack Obama's mother is white and his father was black. Barack tends to carry more of the father gene features due to the higher reservoir of energy the melanin carries, and less of an energy reservoir of his white mother's genes. The lower energy reservoir within the genes of a particular racial group, the higher percentage of skin cancer compared to those with higher energy.

Melanin is a dominant gene. You can't get genetically recessive to blacks whose genes are dominant. Black Africans possessed genes to produce all varieties and races of men. Black to black can produce any color. You can't get black from white, but you can get white from black due to the higher Emotional Reservoir.

Table 3
*Worldwide Average Differences Among Blacks, Whites, and East Asians*

| Trait | Blacks | Whites | East Asians |
|---|---|---|---|
| Intelligence | | | |
| IQ test scores | 85 | 102 | 106 |
| Decision times | Slower | Intermediate | Faster |
| Cultural achievements | Low | High | High |
| Brain size | | | |
| Cranial capacity (cm³) | 1,267 | 1,347 | 1,364 |
| Cortical neurons (millions) | 13,185 | 13,665 | 13,767 |
| Maturation rate | | | |
| Gestation time | Shorter | Longer | Longer |
| Skeletal development | Earlier | Intermediate | Later |
| Motor development | Earlier | Intermediate | Later |
| Dental development | Earlier | Intermediate | Later |
| Age of first intercourse | Earlier | Intermediate | Later |
| Age of first pregnancy | Earlier | Intermediate | Later |
| Life span | Shortest | Intermediate | Longest |
| Personality | | | |
| Aggressiveness | Higher | Intermediate | Lower |
| Cautiousness | Lower | Intermediate | Higher |
| Impulsivity | Higher | Intermediate | Lower |
| Self-concept | Higher | Intermediate | Lower |
| Sociability | Higher | Intermediate | Lower |
| Reproduction | | | |
| Two-egg twinning (per 1,000 births) | 16 | 8 | 4 |
| Hormone levels | Higher | Intermediate | Lower |
| Sex characteristics | Larger | Intermediate | Smaller |
| Intercourse frequencies | Higher | Intermediate | Lower |
| Permissive attitudes | Higher | Intermediate | Lower |
| Sexually transmitted diseases | Higher | Intermediate | Lower |
| Social organization | | | |
| Marital stability | Lower | Intermediate | Higher |
| Law abidingness | Lower | Intermediate | Higher |
| Mental health | Lower | Intermediate | Higher |

*Note.* From *Race, Evolution, and Behavior: A Life History Perspective* (p. 5), by J. P. Rushton, 2000, Port Huron, MI: Charles Darwin Research Institute. Copyright 2000 by J. P. Rushton. Adapted with permission.

The chart above illustrates that where blacks' scores are higher, are areas that are caused or associated with higher Emotional Reservoir. Excluding other foolishness, like first intercourse, etc.

This data was presented by Professor Ruston, who believed that testosterone is the master switch that sets the position of the races. He believes that with higher testosterone levels, blacks are more likely to possess more energy than other races, which can also contribute to aggression and behavior problems. In his book *Race, Evolution, and Behavior* – Chart 3 *(Black Infants Develop*

*Physically Sooner than Other Infants),* Ruston posits that black babies mature more quickly than whites, while Orientals mature more slowly. He also believes that black babies are not born prematurely; they are born sooner, but biologically they are more mature. The length of pregnancy depends on the genes. [4]

Ruston recognized these physical differences but failed to provide further explanation of what causes such differences in the black genes.

The Western mainstream psychologists have failed to recognize any other form of intelligence outside their "own comfort box" of IQ (Intelligent Quotient), or left-brained as valid intelligence. Like many Western psychologists, Professor Ruston believes that based on scientific studies, blacks are less intelligent than whites in IQ, and the reason is genetic. During a speech Ruston gave at the American Renaissance Conference in the year 2000, an attendant asked him: "How come blacks in Haiti that he believes to have lower IQ, were able to defeat the Napoleon army?"

He responded that it was "absolutely a puzzle, an unsolved puzzle. Maybe African lower IQ is different in meaning somehow from that of white IQ."

If we are to agree with Professor Ruston that lower IQ is different in meaning to that of white high IQ, then why haven't Western psychologists studied what that "different" means before coming to their conclusions in regards to human intelligence? Or questioned why whites and Orientals possess less Emotional Reservoir than blacks who tend to have more of this intelligence?

Western psychologists failed to recognize these so-called "black traits" as some form of intelligence. Even Daniel Goleman failed to recognize this so-called "black trait" as Emotional Intelligence that blacks possess more than other races.

One thing for sure is that when it comes to Emotional Intelligence whites are not too keen to know or worried about what race may have more of this intelligence. Western psychologists seem to turn a blind eye and remain completely oblivious when it comes to African intelligence. Why?

I believe that there has been a worldwide attempt in psychology to refute any study that might reveal the true CORE of intelligence without sabotaging what Western mainstream psychologists believe. If we are to study true human intelligence, we must study intelligence across the spectrum, not just highlighting what gives Westerners advantage over others. If we judge one thing based on its areas of expertise, then we are leaving a huge portion of intelligence out there undiscovered.

For example, just because a woman tends to rely more on her emotions, does that make her less intelligent? But since we live in a man's world, everything has to be measured by IQ. So, Africans, Native Americans and other isolated tribes of the world who rely more on emotional connection than IQ, are looked down upon as inferior by those who don't understand the essence of human emotion.

My theory suggests that some people tend to use more of a certain part of the brain compared to others, depending on the geographical climate where they evolved and the challenges they might have faced during their evolutionary process. One person may be a carpenter and be excellent at working with wood; another person may be a physics professor and be excellent at remembering formulas and figuring out mathematical relationships. I would say that both of these people are intelligent, in their own way.

In this chapter, I serve as a guide in a journey through a new paradigm that urges us to harmonize head and heart. A voyage aimed at bringing greater understanding to some of the most perplexing moments in our own lives and in the world around us.[5] It is with the heart that one sees rightly; what is essential is invisible to the eyes.[6] To do what is well in our lives means we must first understand more exactly what it means to use emotion intelligently.

Scientists have told us that humans first developed the emotional brain many years before the left-brain, which is referred to as the thinking brain. To better grasp the potent hold of the emotions on the thinking mind, and why feeling and reason are so readily at war, consider how the brain evolved. The emotional centers emerged from the most primitive root, the brainstem. The most ancient root of our emotional life is in the sense of smell, or more precisely, in the olfactory lobe – the cells that take in and analyze smell. Every living entity – be it nutritious, poisonous, sexual partner, predator or prey – has a distinctive molecular signature that can be carried in the wind.

In those primitive times, smell commended itself as a paramount sense for survival. From the olfactory lobe, the ancient centers for emotion began to evolve. As it evolved, the limbic system refined two power tools: learning and memory. The connections between the olfactory bulb and the limbic system now took on the tasks of making distinctions among smells and recognizing them, comparing a present smell with past ones, and so discriminating good from bad.

Millions of years later in evolution, from these emotional areas evolved the thinking brain or the "neocortex". The neocortex is the seat of thought; it contains the centers that put together and comprehend what the senses perceive. It adds to a feeling what we think about it, and allows us to have feelings about ideas, art, symbols, and imaginings. The survival edge is due to the neocortex's talent for strategizing, long-term planning, and other mental wiles. Beyond that, triumphs of civilization and culture are all fruits of the neocortex.

The fact that the thinking brain grew from the emotional, reveals much about the relationship of thought to feeling; there was an emotional brain long before there was a rational one.

The emotional brain plays a crucial role in the neural architecture. As the root from which the newer brain grew, the emotional areas are intertwined via myriad connecting circuits to lay all parts of the neocortex. This gives the emotional centers immense power to influence the functioning of the rest of the brain, including its centers of thought. [7]

In the brain's architecture, the amygdala is the specialist for emotional matters. If the amygdala is severed from the rest of the brain, the result is a striking inability to measure the emotional significance of events. In humans, the amygdala is an almond-shaped cluster of interconnected structures perched above the brainstem, near the bottom of the limbic ring. There are two amygdales – one on each side of the brain, situated towards the side of the head. Amygdala acts as a storehouse of emotional memory. All passion depends on it and is thus of significance itself; life without amygdala is a life stripped of personal meanings.

The neuroscientist Joseph LeDoux explains that the amygdala can control what we do even as the thinking brain, the neocortex, is still coming to a decision.[8] This means that our emotions have a mind of their own, one which can hold quite independently of the rational mind.[9] Incoming signals from the senses let the amygdala scan every experience for trouble. This puts the amygdala in a powerful post for mental life, something like a psychological sentinel, challenging every situation, every perception. It questions the mind: "Is this something I hate? That hurts me? Something I fear?"

If the moment at hand somehow draws a "Yes", the amygdala reacts instantaneously, like a neural tripwire, telegraphing a message of crisis to all parts of the brain. The amygdala is a bit like an alarm company where operators stand ready to send out emergency calls to the fire department, police, and neighbors, whenever a home security system signals trouble. [10]

During evolution, the emotional mind was our "radar for danger". If we waited for rational mind to judge, we might be dead! For the rational mind, it takes a moment or two longer to register and respond than it does the emotional mind. In every situation, the "first impulse" is the heart's, not the head's. As we see, the emotional mind is far quicker at reading reality in an instant, making the intuitive snap and judgment that tells us who to be wary of, who to trust, and who's in distress.[11]

The advantage of emotional intelligence is the power of creativity and intuitive ability which helps to have a positive attitude towards life, to understand the perspective of others, and to be successful in things like music, sport, entertainment, and dancing. In the emotional repertoire, each emotion plays a unique role, as revealed by their distinctive biological signatures.[12] Researchers continue to argue over precisely which emotions can be considered primary. There are hundreds of emotions, along with their blends, variation, and mutation. Indeed, there are more subtleties of emotion than we have words for.[13]

The very root of the word Emotion is *motere,* the Latin verb "to move"[14], which literally means energy in motion. In itself, emotional energy is neutral. It is the feeling, sensation, and physiological reaction that makes a specific emotion positive or negative. All emotions are, in essence, impulses to act, the instant plans for handling life that evolution has installed in us.

According to Socrates, sensations are given at birth[15] which is why newborn babies have intense feelings from the moment they are born.[16] Children first develop Emotional Intelligence way before they can fully understand logical intelligence. In so:

> *"To deny our own impulses is to deny the*
> *very thing that makes us human."*

Given the above characterization of knowledge, there are many ways that one might come to know something. Knowledge of empirical facts about the physical world will necessarily involve perception – in other words, the use of the senses. A lot of our mundane knowledge comes from the senses, as we look, smell, taste, and touch the various objects in our environments. Also, all knowledge requires some amount of reasoning to analyze what our senses tell us. Once knowledge is obtained, it can be sustained and passed onto others. Memory allows us to know something that we knew in the past, even perhaps if we no longer remember the original justification.

Knowledge can also be transmitted from one individual to another via testimony. This concept of "knowing" has been with Africans since the beginning of time. Throughout history, African people practiced and understood that knowledge comes from their abilities to use their intuitive power. With this, they were able to start civilization and live in harmony with nature for many years. For example: in the first few milliseconds of perceiving something, Africans not only unconsciously comprehend what it is, but decide whether they like it or not; the cognitive unconscious presents our awareness with not just the identity of what we see, but an opinion about it.[17]

Based on the theory of evolution, Charles Darwin believed that Africa was the "the cradle of mankind". Modern humans evolved in Africa about 200,000 years ago. Africans and non-Africans then split about 100,000 years ago. Orientals and Whites split about 40,000 years ago.[18] The further north the people went "out of Africa", the harder it was to get food, gain shelter, make clothes, and raise children.

In order to live longer and survive in harsh weather with life-threatening challenges, the group which evolved into today's white European and Orientals had to develop a system whereby reason was freed of the pull of emotion. This is because environment dictates intelligence. Africa, Europe, and Asia had very different climates and geographies that called for different skills, resource usage, and lifestyles.

Blacks evolved in a tropical climate, which contrasted with the cooler one of Europe in which whites evolved, and even more so with the cold Arctic lands where Orientals evolved.[19] Critical thinking increased the chances of survival in harsh winter environments, and was able to help in the task of lifting them out of the darkness of the caves.[20] So, the groups that left Africa had to develop certain skills, techniques, and behavior out of survival, which weren't needed in tropical Africa.

As a result of the environmental challenges they encountered during the evolutionary process, they had no choice but to capitalize fully on the left-brain. Europeans and Asian tend to use this part of the brain more. For example, one must require logic to withstand a climate where it is difficult to cultivate due to the cold winter weather and snow. To survive, they had to shed animal skin to make clothes, and to preserve food, the flesh meat was stored under the snow. Africa didn't need to survive under a tropical environment.

For Africans, it was very important to stay connected to nature. They understood that in order for a man to live in peace and to experience inner knowledge, he must listen to the heart in order for him to become fully "one" with the universe. The tradition embraces every individual's intuition abilities to spring out; this invisible driving force has helped black people to thrive throughout the history of human evolution, helping them to create the first musical instruments, farming tools, culture, and music.

Through this knowledge, they lived happily with one another, free from war, conflict, and stress. So, they rejected anything outside these spiritual connections. They specialized in the act of hunting; they cultivated and harvested their own food. After harvest, they would gather around and send thanks to the god of the land for having made it possible for them. They would sing and dance, as these helped them to stay attuned and in alignment with the divine forces, and also helped serve as form of communication with the gods. Their music carries a lot of emotional and spiritual energy, because they understood that everything in the universe operates in forms of energy; even life itself is a form of energy.

For example, even today, some Africans still celebrate the Yam Festival as an annual cultural carnival held at the end of the rainy seasons. Usually at the beginning of the festival, the yams are offered to gods and ancestors first, before distributing them to the village. The ritual is performed either by the oldest man in the community or by the king. This man also offers the yams to God, deities, and ancestors, by showing gratitude to God for His protection and kindness in leading them from lean periods to the time of bountiful harvest, without deaths resulting from hunger. After the prayer of thanksgiving to God, they eat the first yam because it is believed that their position bestows the privilege of being intermediaries between their communities and the gods of the land. This festival is also an occasion for music and display, for the luxury of expensive gowns and cloaks, followed by cultural dances by men, women, and children. This ceremony features brilliant activities, contemporary shows, and fashion parades of great umbrellas twirling above the head of the chiefs.

The very core of African people's knowledge is their intuition ability, which is why they are deeply spiritual people and connected to nature. Africans are very optimistic. This great motivator means that they have a strong expectation that, in general, things will turn out all right in life. From the standpoint of this emotional intelligence, optimism and hope are the attitude that buffers blacks against falling into apathy, hopelessness, or depression despite tough goings.[21]

The social skills black people possess contribute to their ability to understand other people and include the capacity to discern and respond appropriately to the moods, temperaments, motivations, and desires of other people.[22] For emotionally intelligent people, life holds meaning for them. They tend to be assertive, express their feelings appropriately, and adapt well to stress. They feel positive about themselves; their social poise lets them easily reach out to new people.[23]

For Africans, all meaningful reality was rooted in the spirituality and emotion connection. And further, if you have intuitions at all, they come from a deeper nature than the loquacious level which rationalism inhabits. Your whole subconscious life, your impulses, your faiths, your needs, your divinations, have prepared the promises which your consciousness now feels, and something in you absolutely knows that the result must be true. [24]

This explains why Ancient Africa was a continent of wealthy and powerful civilizations and empires, such as the Mali Empire, the

Benin Empire, the Kingdom of Ashanti, the Great Zimbabwe, and many more. The Mali Empire grew rich on trade, and at its peak it was one of the jewels of the African continent, known all over the world for its wealth and luxury.

One legendary story about the kingdom's riches concerns the ruler Mansa Musa, who stopped over in Egypt during a fourteenth century pilgrim to Mecca. Musa dished out so much gold during the visit that he caused its value to plummet in the Egyptian market for several years. Timbuktu was an intellectual and spiritual capital and home of the first, most prestigious university in the world, which included a library with estimated collections of 700.000 manuscripts. The collections included manuscripts about art, medicine, philosophy, and science, as well as copies of the Quran.[25]

Traditionally, African kings had no political function. Their role was spiritual or supernatural – to mediate between the cosmological forces: the sky, the earth, and the sea, each of which is represented by a god. The King's role is to propitiate these gods and maintain harmony among them. If the sky god is "angry", there will be thunder, heavy downpour, floods, etc. That would mean the king had failed to perform his function.

In various African traditional governance systems – such as, Ashanti of Ghana, the Igbo of Nigeria, the Somali, the Tswana of Botswana, the Shona of Zimbabwe, the Xhosa, and the Zulu of South Africa – the King and Chiefs in Council discuss all matters of political and judicial administration. A chief was chosen by the Queen Mother of the royal family to rule for life; the Council of Elders, which consists of heads of extended families in the village, must ratify his appointment with constitutional checks and balance to prevent abuse of power:

*"We do not wish for greediness*
*We do not wish that his ears should be hard of hearing*
*We do not wish that he should act on his own initiative."*

The Chief must consult with the Council on all-important matters. Without this Council, the Chief is powerless. For instance, if despots arose, they were dethroned as soon as they could.

Between ruler and people there was acknowledged recognition of ties of mutual obligation and respect.[26] For the Africans, if actually examined, this provides an exact parallel with the European regna, and in almost exactly the same historical time.[27] Centralized power, at least within the limits of human frailty, was exercised within structures that were devolutionary in their intention and usually in their effect. Europeans who first came in close contact with the Ashanti, increasingly in the nineteenth century, certainly wrote of Ashanti as a nation-state, because it had all the attributes that justified the label. It had a given territory, known territorial limits, a central government with police and army, a national language and law, and, beyond these, a constitutional embodiment in the form of a council, called the Ashantiman. This was a kind of parliament, according to a British observer in 1886.[28]

What this says is that these communities achieved an accountability of rulers to rule and, quite persistently, the other way around as well. For centuries, these societies were successful in mastering their historical process, and were centrally concerned in securing and sustaining their legitimacy in the eyes of their people. They endured because they were accepted. And they were accepted because their rules of operation were found to be sufficiently reasonable in providing explanation, and sufficiently persuasive in extracting obedience. [29]

The Africans didn't need to develop a behavior based on survival, because they had everything they needed. They had good weather, fertile land, gold, silver, diamonds, and many other natural resources. Europeans, on the other hand, were acting based on survival, as they needed food, cotton, and tea, and many other things. They became travelers and explorers, sailing across the world looking for foods, sugar cane, gold, tea, and other natural resources.

Westerners are intolerant of other ways to organize society and other ways to be human. They cannot accept that others may value different ways of being, and different ways of learning. They seem to be stuck in the idea that all people must want what they have and what they value – all those things that they believe prove that Western civilization is the pinnacle of human achievement, the best.[30]

Consequently, from these European behaviors came colonization of Africa and slavery. Engaging in warfare with those whose lands and resources they wanted and who they considered to be inferior because they had a different way of living.

Today, Africans are spread all across the globe; the bond to the motherland was broken and spirituality disrupted. For years, I have visited many parts of Africa and I have become acutely aware of what we have lost. I was deeply saddened by what I believed was an irreparable loss. Today, across the African continent and the world, we find blacks in the haste to have a world entirely based on artificial – that means man-made – things. They have thrown away much that is part of their heritage as creatures of this planet. By divorcing themselves from nature, they have also removed themselves from the wisdom that comes from their ancestors.[31] We rejected age-old knowledge of the riches of the earth that are freely available all around us. In the rush to possess man-made, non-living things, like money, cars, houses, computers, and gadgets, we have ignored our talents and abilities we have in our genes. It seems that all such knowledge was erased by the intolerance of other-ness.[32]

Not long ago, most people – almost all people – had few choices they could make. A thousand years ago, people did not have to choose what they ate. They ate what they could find or catch. They did not have to choose who to marry, what race or where to live, or how many children they must have, or choose between which races was more intelligent.

Choosing has become the quintessential aspect of Western society. They call this mad dance *freedom*. They are listening to expert advice. All too often they find, twenty years later, that the experts were no more expert than they were, that they too were ignorant.

They are proud to be a society of *free* people, by which we mean people who are free to choose, people who, in fact, *must* choose – endlessly, all day – often making choices from alternatives that are so new that they have not had time even to imagine the consequences.

They are choosing in a fog. Our world has become a world of chaotic over-abundance and we feel stressed. The stresses we feel are in large part the result of the overwhelming number of alternatives we must choose from, but also the result of the fact that we have had no time to develop an ethic to help us choose. The headlong rush into new technologies and new ideas, without the time to consider the consequences, makes it almost impossible for us to choose. How can we have an opinion about something that did not exist yesterday? Most ancient cultures of the world did not choose often, if at all; life was what was in front of you. [33]

According to the German philosopher Jean Gebser in his book *The Structures of Consciousness,* he wrote that each structure of consciousness goes through a period of development, at the end of which it enters what he calls its "deficient mode". This is when what was initially an asset becomes a handicap, when the potentials of a structure have been exhausted, and when the characteristics associated with a consciousness structure atrophy and harden into exaggerations of themselves. This development is necessary in order for the next consciousness structure to emerge. The previous one needs to break up so it can make space for the new structure.

He believed that we are living through the last stages of the deficient mode of the mental-rational structure, and he believed that within a few decades, a "global catastrophe" was, if not imminent, certainly very likely. This is the result of left-brain aggression.[34] The Western left-brain idea of societies can only go on as long it can control and create division, and manipulate others for its own selfish gain for the few at the top.

As Africans, we must develop a new system, a Utopia, and find ways to heal old wounds, re-build our emotional connections with our ancestors, and reconnect with our spirituality. Perhaps, despite great destruction of human experience, ancient insight and wisdom are not lost. Somehow, they are still part of us, inside us. These insights can and will come back to us when we need them.

In order for Utopia to come into existence, a bridge has to be built and spiritual transformation must take place in our body, mind, and soul towards the process of reconciliation between Africans and African-American people. The step requires a spiritual healing to heal the error of generational pains and solitude both Africans and African-Americans hold within themselves. Both of these people must learn to regain trust from each other, regain a "sense of urgency", have an open dialogue to discuss the past trauma about slavery, and mourn the loss of the souls of the innocent ancestors. As the healing process advances, there must be legal and international laws that protect these bonds.

After this has taken place, one must reconcile with the other by working together towards building of the bridge and the creation of African Utopia. The success of African Utopia will depend on how strong the spiritual tie is with the African-Americans. The "survival" of African-Americans will depend on how connected they are with their African brothers and sisters, and with the motherland of Africa.

A Reconciliation Treaty must be drawn up within the African Union that will give the African-American people the right to abode and reside in any nation state within sub-Saharan Africa. Under the reconciliation agreement of the government of whichever state and place they choose to reside, they must be protected and provided with clear information that will permit them and enable them to resettle back into their motherland. They must be given clarity on where and how they can acquire land, where they can grow their own food or build a home. And be given an opportunity to serve within various governmental positions.

Black music is the secret key to the passage that connects us with our spirituality; it should not be allowed to be sensitized to the point that it loses its essence and meaning. As we have already seen in history, when we let someone else control our music, they tend to distort the very importance of black music which is its spirituality and emotional value. The effect of this distortion causes an emotional, unbalanced dissonance in our psyche, body, and soul. If we continue to consume those same types of distorted genres of music, this can cause violent behavior.

We must not let ourselves be misled again and manipulated by those who find our emotions a sign of weakness they can walk upon. We must learn when to use our emotional power and when not to use it.

Blacks must balance their emotion and develop it to mastery in order for them to live a happier and fulfilling life. Before one unlashes his anger and frustration on other men, women, or children, he must remember that whatever emotion he unleashes on the next person – positive or negative – will radiate back to him, his community, and neighbour. Energy doesn't die, but transfers to the next person.

If we are to have an organized country, community, and family, it is vital we start with balancing this Emotional Reservoir. Teaching black children how to use their emotional intelligence will be more effective than having a higher IQ. As Africans, we are raised to believe that beating and punishing children helps to keep them disciplined. But this is far from the truth. It is like adding kerosene to a burning flame, so instead we must help them to balance this energy by simply helping them to understand their emotions and how to use them to prevent being emotionally unbalanced.

I believe that if we introduce Emotional Intelligence into the school curriculum, we can reduce the high percentage of the crimes and behavioral issues found amongst the black communities. Once we learn to master our Emotional Reservoir problems such as aggression, anger, impulsiveness and jealousy, then envy and hate will also decrease.

# NOTES

## My Childhood Days

1. *Economic history of Nigeria*, Wikipedia.org
2. Carter G. Woodson, *The Mis-Education of The Negro, The seat of the trouble*, published 1933 pp.2.

## Journey to Pan-Africanism

1. Alex Haley and Malcolm X, *The Autobiography of Malcolm X*, Satan, published 1965 pp.256.
2. Ibid. pp. 256- 257.
3. Ibid. pp. 270.
4. Ibid. El-hajj Malik El-Shabazz, pp. 465.
5. Kwame Nkrumah, *I Speak Of Freedom*, 1961, Wikipedia.org
6. Carter G. Woodson, *The Mis-Education of The Negro, Hirelings In Public Servants' Places*, published 1933 pp.122.
7. Alex Haley and Malcolm X, *The Autobiography of Malcolm X*, Icarus, published 1965 pp. 390.
8. Hitler's with an Introduction by D. C. Watt, *Mein Kampf, A Reckoning*, published 1969 pp. 270-271.
9. Carter G. Woodson, *The Mis-Education of The Negro, Hirelings In Public Servants' Places*, published 1933 pp.123.
10. Hitler's with an Introduction by D. C. Watt, *Mein Kampf, A Reckoning*, published 1969 pp. 272.
11. Alex Haley and Malcolm X, *The Autobiography of Malcolm X*, Icarus, publisher 1965 pp. 372-373.
12. Ibid. pp. 381.
13. Ibid. pp. 390-391.
14. Ibid. pp. 381-382.
15. Hitler's with an Introduction by D. C. Watt, *Mein Kampf, A Reckoning*, published 1969 pp. 270.
16. Carter G. Woodson, *The Mis-education of The Negro, Hirelings In Public Servants' Places*, publisher 1933 pp.124.

17. Hitler's with an Introduction by D. C. Watt, *Mein Kampf, A Reckoning*, published 1969 pp. 270.
18. Ibid. pp. 272.
19. Ibid. pp. 269-270.

## Study and Observation

1. Alice Walker, *The Color Purple*, published 1983 pp. 209-210.
2. Urban Dictionary definition of *Big Man Syndrome*: unwillingness to listen or to compromise, unreasonable demands you expect to be fulfilled and belief everyone else shares your interest.
3. Dinesh D' Souza, *The End Of Racism, The White Man's Burden*, published 1995, pp.16.
4. Carter G. Woodson, *The Mis-education of The Negro,* The Seat Of Trouble, published 1933 pp.7.
5. Hitler's with an Introduction by D. C. Watt, *Mein Kampf, A Reckoning*, published 1969 pp. 29.
6. Carter G. Woodson, *The Mis-education of The Negro,* The Seat Of Trouble, published 1933 pp.7.
7. Ibid. Preface pp. xvii
8. Hitler's with an Introduction by D. C. Watt, *Mein Kampf, A Reckoning*, published 1969 pp. 33.
9. Basil Davidson, *The Black Man's Burden Africa And The Curse of The Nation-State,* Africa Without History, published 1992 pp. 35.
10. Ibid. pp. 39.
11. Ibid. pp. 38.
12. Ibid. pp. 41.
13. Ibid. pp.176 [note 9 Basil Davidson] pp. 331.
14. Ibid. pp. 47.
15. Ibid. pp. 40.
16. Carter G. Woodson, *The Mis-education of The Negro,* The Educated Negro, published 1933 pp.61.
17. Hitler's with an Introduction by D. C. Watt, *Mein Kampf, A Reckoning*, published 1969 pp. 140.
18. Ibid. pp. 123.
19. Ibid. pp. 232.

20. Basil Davidson, *The Black Man's Burden Africa And The Curse of The Nation-State,* The Black Man's Burden, published 1992 pp. 205.
21. Ibid. pp. 19.
22. Carter G. Woodson, *The Mis-education of The Negro,* Hirelings In Public Servants' Places, published 1933 pp.125. (*)
23. Basil Davidson, *The Black Man's Burden Africa And The Curse of The Nation-State,* Tribalism And The New Nationalism, published 1992 pp. 108.
24. Ibid. The Black Man's Burden pp. 209.
25. Ibid. The Black Man's Burden pp. 215.
26. Teacher Don't teach me Nonsense, Written By, Composed By - Fela Anikulapo Kuti, Released 1986, Label Mercury
27. Carter G. Woodson, *The Mis-education of The Negro,* The Educated Negro, published 1933 pp.57.
28. Hitler's with an Introduction by D. C. Watt, *Mein Kampf,* A Reckoning, published 1969 pp. 11.
29. Carter G. Woodson, *The Mis-education of The Negro,* Service Rather Than Leadership, published 1933 pp116.
30. Plato, *The Republic,* Translated With An Introduction By Desmond Lee, published 1955 pp. 178.
31. Ibid. pp. 183.
32. Ibid. pp. 186.
33. Ibid. pp. 35.
34. Hitler's with an Introduction by D. C. Watt, *Mein Kampf,* A *Reckoning,* published 1969 pp. 29-30.
35. Ibid. pp. 21-22.
36. Ibid. pp. 96.
37. Ibid. pp. 21.
38. Dinesh D' Souza, *The End Of Racism,* The White Man's Burden, published 1995, pp.18.
39. Hitler's with an Introduction by D. C. Watt, *Mein Kampf,* A *Reckoning,* published 1969, pp. 268.

## Change of Perception

1. Stephen R. Covey, *The 7 Habits of Highly Effective People*, Habit 1 Be Proactive, published 2004, pp. 89.
2. Ibid. pp. 69-70.
3. Ibid. pp. 24
4. Ibid. pp. 70.
5. David J. Schwartz, *The Magic Of Thinking Big*, How To Think Big, published1995, pp. 94.
6. Stephen R. Covey, *The 7 Habits of Highly Effective People*, Inside-Out, published 2004, pp. 24.
7. Ibid
8. Ibid. pp. 29.
9. Ibid. pp. 42.
10. Hitler's with an Introduction by D. C. Watt, *Mein Kampf, A Reckoning*, published 1969, pp. 94.
11. Ibid. pp. 56.
12. Ibid. pp. 28.
13. Ibid. pp. 56.
14. Stephen R. Covey, *The 7 Habits of Highly Effective People*, Habit 1 Be Proactive, published 2004, pp. 70.
15. Hitler's with an Introduction by D. C. Watt, *Mein Kampf, A Reckoning*, published 1969, pp. 102.
16. Stephen R. Covey, *The 7 Habits of Highly Effective People*, Habit 1 Be Proactive, published 2004, pp. 72.
17. Hitler's with an Introduction by D. C. Watt, *Mein Kampf, A Reckoning*, published 1969, pp. 27.
18. Alex Haley and Malcolm X, *The Autobiography of Malcolm X*, 'Homeboy', published 1965 pp. 133.
19. Dinesh D' Souza, *The End Of Racism*, The White Man's Burden, published 1995, pp.16.

## Hunters in a Society of Farmers

1. Marimba Ani (Dona Richards), *Yurugu An African-Centered Critique Of European Cultural Thought And Behavior*, Intracultural Behavior, published 1994, pp. 355.

2. Ibid. Utamawazo: *The Cultural Structuring of Thought*, pp. 103.
3. Ibid. Religion and Ideology, pp. 195.
4. Ibid. Behavior Towards Others, pp. 471.
5. Thom Hartmann, *The Last Hours of Ancient Sunlight, Revised and Updated, iBooks*, pp.132.
6. Marimba Ani (Dona Richards), *Yurugu An African-Centered Critique Of European Cultural Thought And Behavior*, Image of Others, published 1994, pp. 302.
7. Ibid. Image of Others, pp. 304.
8. Ibid
9. Thom Hartmann, *The Last Hours of Ancient Sunlight, Revised and Updated, iBook*, pp.131.
10. Gary Lachman, *The Secret Teachers of the Western World*, iBook, pp.15.
11. Ibid. pp. 14-15.
12. Ibid. pp. 12.
13. Thom Hartmann, *The Last Hours of Ancient Sunlight, Revised and Updated, iBook*, pp.131.
14. Marimba Ani (Dona Richards), *Yurugu An African-Centered Critique Of European Cultural Thought And Behavior*, Aesthetic: The Power of Symbols, published 1994, pp. 203.
15. Ibid. Utamawazo: *The Cultural Structuring of Thought*, pp. 35-38.
16. Ibid. pp. 46-50.
17. Ibid. pp. 43.
18. Ibid. pp. 36.
19. Ibid. pp. 44.
20. Thom Hartmann, *The Last Hours of Ancient Sunlight, Revised and Updated, iBook*, pp.129.
21. Marimba Ani (Dona Richards), *Yurugu An African-Centered Critique Of European Cultural Thought And Behavior*, Utamawazo: *The Cultural Structuring of Thought*, published 1994, pp. 48.
22. Ibid. pp. 37.
23. I bid. pp. 43.
24. Thom Hartmann, *Attention Deficit Disorder, A Different Perception*, Author's Introduction, published 1999, pp. xxvi.
25. Marimba Ani (Dona Richards), *Yurugu An African-Centered Critique Of European Cultural Thought And Behavior*, Utamawazo: The Cultural Structuring of Thought, published 1994, pp. 21-22.

26. Ibid. Introduction by John Henrik Clarke, pp. xvi.

27. Thom Hartmann, *The Last Hours of Ancient Sunlight, Revised and Updated, iBook*, pp.130.

28. Ibid. pp. 129.

29. http://edition.cnn.com/2008/POLITICS/04/28/wright.transcript/

30. Marimba Ani (Dona Richards), *Yurugu An African-Centered Critique Of European Cultural Thought And Behavior*, Introduction by John Henrik Clarke, pp.xvi.

31. Ibid. Introduction, pp.19.

32. Gary Lachman, *The Secret Teachers of the Western World*, iBook, pp.22.

33. Ibid. 21.

34. Thom Hartmann, *Attention Deficit Disorder, A Different Perception*, Author's Introduction, published 1999, pp. xxxv-xxx.

35. http://edition.cnn.com/2008/POLITICS/04/28/wright.transcript/

36. Thom Hartmann, *The Last Hours of Ancient Sunlight, Revised and Updated, iBook*, pp.130.

37. Ibid.

38. Ibid. pp.128.

39. Gary Lachman, *The Secret Teachers of the Western World*, iBook, pp.15.

40. Thom Hartmann, *The Last Hours of Ancient Sunlight, Revised and Updated, iBook*, pp.18.

41. Ibid. pp.19.

## Emotional Reservoir

1. Daniel Goleman, *Emotional Intelligence, Why it can matter more than IQ*, Aristotle's Challenge, published 1996, pp. ix.

2. J. Philippe Rushton, *Race, Evolution, and Behavior, a Life History Perspective*, Race Is More Than Skin Deep, published 1995, pp. 7.

3. Ibid.

4. Ibid. pp.13.

5. Daniel Goleman, *Emotional Intelligence, Why it can matter more than IQ*, Aristotle's Challenge, published 1996, pp. xii.

6. Ibid. What are emotions for? pp.3.

7. Ibid. pp.10-12.

8. Ibid. pp.14.

9. Ibid. pp.20.

10. Ibid. pp.16.

11. Ibid. Appendix B, pp.292-293.

12. Ibid. What are emotions for? pp.6.

13. Ibid. Appendix A, pp.289.

14. Ibid. What are emotions for? pp.6.

15. Marimba Ani (Dona Richards), *Yurugu An African-Centered Critique Of European Cultural Thought And Behavior*, Utamawazo: The Cultural Structuring of Thought, published 1994, pp. 43.

16. Daniel Goleman, *Emotional Intelligence, Why it can matter more than IQ, Schooling Emotions*, published 1996, pp. 273.

17. Ibid. Anatomy of an Emotional Hijacking, pp.20.

18. J. Philippe Rushton, *Race, Evolution, and Behavior, a Life History Perspective,* Out of Africa, published 1995, pp. 39.

19. Ibid. pp.12.

20. Marimba Ani (Dona Richards), *Yurugu An African-Centered Critique Of European Cultural Thought And Behavior*, Utamawazo: The Cultural Structuring of Thought, published 1994, pp. 53.

21. Daniel Goleman, *Emotional Intelligence, Why it can matter more than IQ,* The Master Aptitude, published 1996, pp. 88

22. Ibid. The nature of Emotional Intelligence, pp.39.

23. Ibid. When Smart Is Dumb, pp.45.

24. Marimba Ani (Dona Richards), *Yurugu An African-Centered Critique Of European Cultural Thought And Behavior*, Religion and Ideology, published 1994, pp.182.

25. https://en.m.wikipedia.org

26. Basil Davidson, *The Black Man's Burden Africa And The Curse of The Nation-State,* The Road Not Taken, published 1992 pp. 60-61.

27. Ibid. Shadows Of Neglected Ancestors, pp.92.

28. Ibid. The Road Not Taken, pp.60.

29. Ibid. Shadows Of Neglected Ancestors, pp.88.

30. Robert Wolff, *Original Wisdom, Stories of an Ancient Way of Knowing,* Introduction, Copyright 2001, pp. 4-5.

31. Ibid. Introduction, pp.2.
32. Ibid. Introduction, pp.5.
33. Ibid. Draw Something, Anything pp.21-23.
34. Gary Lachman, *The Secret Teachers of the Western World*, iBook, pp.25.

Lightning Source UK Ltd.
Milton Keynes UK
UKHW041509310719
347150UK00001B/94/P